PROFITIN(YOUR PRI[

Users' Guide to Computer Printing

by Frank Booty

LINCOLNSHIRE
COUNTY COUNCIL

004.77

ComputerWeekly

Published by Computer Weekly Publications,
Quadrant House, The Quadrant, Sutton, Surrey SM2 5AS

Publications Manager: John Riley
Deputy Publications Manager: Robin Frampton
Publications Assistant: Katherine Canham

 © 1990

British Library Cataloguing in Publication Data

   Booty, Frank
   Profiting from your printer: users' guide to computer printing.
   1. Computer systems. Printers
   I. Title 004.77
   ISBN 1-85384-019-X

All rights reserved. No part of this publication may be reproduced, stored in a retrieval system, or transmitted, in any form or by any means, electronic, mechanical, photocopying, recording and/or otherwise, without the prior written permission of the publishers

Printed by Hobbs The Printers, Southampton

CONTENTS

Acknowledgements		iv
Foreword		v
Introduction		vi
Chapter 1	Printer Technologies	1
Chapter 2	Buying a Printer	21
Chapter 3	Connecting a Printer to Your System	41
Chapter 4	Desktop Publishing and Networking	69
Chapter 5	Paper Handling	83
Chapter 6	Accessories and Consumables - the Hidden Costs	97
Chapter 7	Printer Maintenance and Servicing	107
Chapter 8	The Different Types of Printer	121
Chapter 9	Which Printer for a Particular Application?	137
Appendix 1	Quick Price Guide	169
Appendix 2	Manufacturers' Names and Addresses	173
Glossary of Commonly-Used Printer Jargon		185
Index		195

ACKNOWLEDGEMENTS

In writing this book, aside from nearly going mad, I drew upon the experience and knowledge of many colleagues and contacts, as well as key representatives within many printer manufacturers and consultancies. While there is not space enough to mention them all, I would like to make particular reference to colleagues and staff working for (in no particular order) Hermes, Kyocera, Epson, IBM, ICL, Granada, Printer World, Hewlett-Packard, Genicom, Canon and Romtec, for their assistance in compiling this tome.

Most of all, I'd like to acknowledge the patience of my wife and family - Julia, Adam and Oliver - for putting up with me during the preparation of the manuscript.

FOREWORD

Considerable time and effort generally goes into evaluating and selecting a computer system, whether for personal or office use. However, all too often the bulk of that effort goes into choosing the computer itself. The printer becomes an afterthought, with insufficient attention paid to the use to which it will be put.

This is paradoxical because the printer is the key interface between the user and the system, and the right choice of printer is crucial for ensuring a smooth-running application.

As well as a guide to choosing a printer, this book also concentrates heavily on cost-effective usage of that printer. It draws attention to hidden costs, explains how to maximise the use of the printer, and provides general hints and tips to help prolong the life of the printer and to enhance its efficiency.

The book is essential, not only for those thinking about buying a computer system, but also for those using a system as a checklist for key points to consider when reviewing their printer requirements.

The book fits comfortably into ***Computer Weekly***'s series of books aimed at the new breed of businessperson who is responsible for managing or using computers as a normal part of daily business. The book provides the practical level of synthesis that is so hard to find among the plethora of computer industry information.

John Riley
Publications Manager
Computer Weekly Publications

INTRODUCTION

Buyers sometimes baulk at spending much on a printer

For too long, the area of printers has been neglected to the extent that users will buy any printer without giving any thought to the purchase, other than the cost. Thousands of pounds may have been spent on buying the computer system, but when it comes to the printer, buyers sometime baulk at spending more than a few hundred pounds. This book is intended to be of use to people who find themselves caught in this trap.

This book will help computer users to choose the printer(s) best suited for the particular application they have in mind. Although it considers printers for systems ranging from the standalone personal computer up to the large mainframe complexes, it will be of maximum benefit to users of PCs and mid-range systems, especially those who are not particularly computer literate.

The book is structured so that chapters and sections of chapters can be taken and studied in standalone fashion, so that the first-time PC user will gain as much insight as, say, a first-time users of a multi-terminal system where that user is actually a 350-strong company.

Existing users will gain useful tips and, indeed, may decide to change their computer system configurations to incorporate different printers.

It should be remembered that with the fast-moving state of technology, some of the products and even one of the technologies mentioned in this book could soon become out-of-date (but not obsolete). Whatever happens in the world of information technology, you will still be able to use the information in this book, if only for conceptual data and guidance.

STRUCTURE OF BOOK

Starting from the basic concepts, the book takes you from the analytical stage of working out what type of printer is best suited for your application, right through to outlining what makes of machine might best do the job. This is a particularly sensitive area as no-one can claim to provide the definite answer to your needs. Also specific models are constantly being updated and new ones introduced and the book should be read with this mind. The book provides a benchmark as of early 1990. Therefore details of specific printers are provided for guidance and reference. It should not be used as the only criterion for purchasing a particular printer.

The bulk of the book comprises chapters detailing how to connect a printer to your system and why certain approaches have to be, or have been, adopted; switching between serial and parallel port connections; considering the intelligent functions built into the latest machines; a look at third/fourth party maintenance aspects, including some cautionary tales; considerations of the various mechanical aspects such as paper handling, form feeding, etc; the hidden costs of printer ownership, including such items as paper quality, print ribbons, cartridges, toner, printer stands, acoustic hoods, etc; desk top publishing - what it is and what it isn't; the impact of the growth of networking on printers; and an overview of the different technologies used in printers today.

FIRST DEMONSTRATION

Selecting a printer can be traumatic. There are lots to choose from, in a variety of different technologies, each suited to different applications, but not one suited to all. Also, you have to ensure that the printer is compatible with your computer's software, and you have to be aware of the running costs.

However, all too often, when a customer is given a demonstration of a computer system, the primary concerns are not to do with printing. They relate to the software, the computer's capability, maintenance programme and, increasingly, ergonomics. Usually, the decision to buy may be made after seeing a full demonstration run on the computer's display screen alone.

The printer is usually treated as an afterthought, and is rarely demonstrated in action. The question you should then ask, if or when you find yourself in this position, is: 'Show me how easy it is to use'.

The responses to these questions may prove surprising. But you can gauge where you stand from the reactions you will get. This book will provide ammunition for more questions like this.

PRICING AND COSTS

Prices are quoted, particularly in Chapter 9. The intention is not to enable the reader to make firm purchasing decisions - as of course the prices will change rapidly. They have been included to give an idea of relative pricing structures and relative costs.

CHAPTER 1

PRINTER TECHNOLOGIES

OVERVIEW

A basic grasp of the differing printer technologies is useful when getting to grips with the pros and cons of various types of printers in differing applications.

Printing technologies split into two camps: impact and non-impact. There are many pros and cons for both sides, the main and most often quoted advantages being noise and multi-part forms capability.

Examples of other considerations are that a non-impact printer will generally be quieter than an impact printer although an impact one will handle anything up to, say, seven part forms in one pass of the printhead. The non-impact device can only produce one copy at a time (so, if you want seven forms you have to run the same page seven times, which means seven times the normal print time, higher costs of consumables, etc).

A non-impact printer will generally be quieter than an impact printer but can only produce one copy at a time

So, that aside, let's look at each technology used today, in no particular order and with no particular preference.

MATRIX, IMPACT

> **IMPACT DOT MATRIX**
> Matrix printers bang a set of needles through a ribbon. Characters are built up successively (i.e. serially) from the pattern of dots as the print head containing the needles moves across the paper
>
> This is still the most common kind of printer, and the basic workhorse for general purpose office use. Quality, especially on the 24-pin printers, is becoming increasingly more acceptable. Running costs are low. Noise remains a problem.

DOT MATRIX

The most common printer technology today is dot matrix. Many of these machines, which seem to sprout just about anywhere you look, are of the long-standing 9-pin vintage. Indeed, conservative estimates point to this group having half of the printer market share. So, as you might expect, there are a lot of people out there trying to sell them, which makes for low prices (ie good news for users but bad news for the profit margins of the manufacturers). Also available are 18, 24 and even 48-pin machines, the first two of which are said to account for some 25 per cent of all matrix printer sales.

There are good reasons for adopting dot matrix technology. It's non-expensive, the costs of running the machines are low and the technology is seasoned and reliable. It's amazing what you can do with the printers too - you can print A3; put in multi-part forms (it's one of the few choices for that application); handle near letter quality (NLQ) text, graphics and draft printing; and handle either cut sheets or fanfold, sprocketed paper.

On the other side of the coin, while the printers will handle cut sheet work, it's not the preferred application. You never get true letter quality either, although 48-pin matrix printers do come close to this. If you can get over the noise (eg by placing the device inside an acoustic hood - which doesn't look very good, but is a cheap way out), and quite high prices for the really fast matrix printers, this technology will be for you.

Dot matrix printers are impact devices, so you are going to get a lot of noise. The printhead is moved across the paper with characters being formed by the pins striking a ribbon, so the resulting image is constituted from a matrix of dots

Dot matrix printers are impact devices. Hence you're going to get a lot of noise. In essence, the printhead - composed of 9, 18, 24 or 48-pins or needles - is moved across the paper with characters being formed by the pins striking a ribbon with a different sequence for each character or symbol. So the resulting image on the paper is constituted from a matrix of dots.

LINE MATRIX

Line matrix printers, which operate in the range 200 to 1,600 lines per minute, differ from the dot matrix printers as outlined above. While the serial devices have printheads with between 9 and 24 closely spaced pins, a line matrix printer has a horizontal array of 24 print hammers on a shuttle, which strike simultaneously, printing a whole line of dots in one sweep. When the sweep is completed, the printer advances the paper one dot row, changes the shuttle direction and prints the next row.

PRINTER TECHNOLOGIES 5

The trade off for the lower speeds available with line matrix printers is the ability to give you graphics. Although the print quality is often pretty dismal, serial dot matrix devices are fast and you can get to work with text or graphics. There's also the bonus of font handling flexibility.

Line matrix printers can give you high resolution graphics in several formats (eg line drawing, block graphics, plotting and bar codes). Also, there's usually a choice of elements such as superscript and subscript, bold type, etc, with some machines adding facilities to mix text, graphics and character pitch in the same print line.

Unlike the serial dot matrix technology, line printing technology has itself advanced nearly as far as it is going to go. About the only things that can happen to these devices are to increase speeds and reduce noise levels.

The line printer market is probably the least vulnerable of all the non-impact technologies, unlike the daisy wheel and dot matrix machines. The reason for this is simple: the applications being addressed by non-impact printers, such as laser printing (letters, desktop publishing, local area networking, etc), where the prime requirement is print quality, are not in the main those addressed by line printers. These are applications that in the past have been taken care of by dot matrix or daisywheel printers (or indeed typewriters).

However, the line matrix market starts at a much lower speed threshold. It is most common to see the entry point around the 200 to 300 lines per minute mark. This is the grey area where many of the dot matrix printer manufacturers can now offer products with similar speeds and much improved graphics capabilities. Line matrix devices can play three aces however: they throw out loads of code, file dumps, etc; they're the only solution for multi-part form printing (the non-impacts are definitely out in the cold on this point); and they can be optimised to handle barcoding and labelling (which is important for point-of-sale applications).

Many of the serial dot matrix printers can also print in colour by the use of a special ribbon. Many also offer the facility to handle one-off cut sheets, so if you're going to need multiple cut sheets, you will need a sheet feeder.

Two modes are to be found usually: the draft mode and near letter quality (NLQ) mode. Draft mode, particularly on a 9-pin printer, can give you an awful printout, but it's acceptable if that's what you expect and all you really need. Invoicing is one such obvious application. For most devices on the market, NLQ isn't strictly near letter quality but it is better and more acceptable than draft output.

The results for NLQ output are usually achieved by the printhead going back over its first print run on the line, giving a dual pass. Indeed it's not unknown for triple pass printing to be offered. Naturally, this form of printing slows the printer considerably, eg a 200 characters per second printer will be slowed to about 50 characters per second.

Choose a 9-pin device if all you really need is draft printing. Machines are marketed which go as fast as 500 characters per second. But if you want near letter quality don't choose a pin-printer - speeds are slow and the quality isn't worth it. Remember that they are the most inexpensive machines, so they do score, if only for that reason.

Choose a 9-pin device if all you really need is draft printing. But if you want near letter quality don't choose a pin-printer as speeds are slow and the quality isn't worth it

Choose 18-pins for draft quality printing at superior speeds to the 9-pin, but again don't buy them for NLQ. They are not worth it.

Choose 24-pins for NLQ output, where you also need draft capability. But don't fall into the trap of thinking this type is for you if you only want to produce letter quality output. The ink jet (see below) is more likely to satisfy you, and keep you within budget.

For applications above the 400 lines per minute range choose line matrix printers. They offer a higher level of sophistication and flexibility than band impact line printers (see below), but with lower speeds.

Whereas serial dot matrix printers are likely to be found in any computer installation, whatever its size and application, be it general offices, dental surgery or clearing bank computer centre, line matrix printers are likely to be found in the traditional computer room or laboratory environment, ie in the professional environment only.

DAISYWHEEL, IMPACT

Arguably the provider of the best letter quality until recently, the daisywheel has reigned supreme above all other printing technologies. Its days may now be numbered, however, particularly with the rise of the laser and the latest ink jet units. Aside from this, the costs of daisywheel printers are very close to those for laser printers, and these are decreasing.

In its favour, daisywheel technology can cite multi-part forms capability, reliability and A3 printing. But it is unfortunately noisy, slow and expensive, and it doesn't offer graphics (or even vertical lines) while many, if not all, users will need a sheet feeder because letter quality work always requires working with cut sheets.

Characters are preformed on the ends of spokes resembling a daisy, and images are transferred to paper by a hammer striking the character against a ribbon. Excellent results are obtained, but as stated above, there's really no advantage other than text capability. This is fine if all you want to output are loads of letters, manuscripts, speeches, etc. Otherwise, look elsewhere to see what technology can provide you with for less cost than the daisywheel.

> **Characters are preformed on the ends of spokes resembling a daisy, and images are transferred to paper by a hammer striking the character against a ribbon. Excellent results are obtained, but there's no other advantage other than text capability**

BAND, IMPACT

> **BAND PRINTERS**
> Band impact printers hit a row of fully-formed characters through a ribbon on to paper. A similar concept to a daisywheel but works a line at a time. Noisy and lacks the ability to print graphics, bar codes or different character sets easily. But band technology is very fast, cheap and still viable for DP use.

The average data-processing department today still churns out loads of paper, mainly the 130 column fan-folded, green-lined variety. Common to many DP rooms is the band printer, a device utilising a technology which has been around for at least eleven years. A steel band embossed with characters thumps out the printed images on a line-by-line basis, while the choice of characters is restricted to straight alphanumerics, with the choice of 48, 64 or 96 characters only. Although they are relatively unsophisticated, they are fast workhorses - some offering speeds of up to 2,000 lines per minute.

While band technology is older and less sophisticated than other technologies, it is less vulnerable to attack from other technologies because most of the band machines operate at speeds in excess of 600 lines per minute. There are not that many printers around that can do the job as fast, particularly for the price.

Generally speaking, if you are looking at the purchase of a band printer, you will probably know a fair bit about computers. You will probably be mainly interested in factors such as the duty cycle, maintenance and servicing. You will also probably know your way around the insides of the printer.

Band printers accounted for some $650 million of revenues in Western Europe in 1988, with a similar expenditure for 1989. Taken with line matrix devices, the market value hovers around $1.1 billion for 1989, which is a sizeable chunk by any standard.

LASER, NON-IMPACT

LASER PRINTERS
Works in a similar way to an office photocopier, fusing a powdered toner to the page. The laser itself is used merely as a scanning light source to build up the image on an electrostatic drum. Toner is then released on to the surface of the drum, transferred electrostatically to the paper, and finally melted on by hot rollers.

Advantages are quietness and speed, and very good quality. The disadvantages are a relatively high purchase price and running costs which although not high are more than the traditional impact matrix and daisywheel technologies. Early worries about the reliability of laser printers appear unfounded. It is the printer of choice for most office applications provided you can afford it.

The low end laser is here to stay. Looking at the printer spectrum, you will find lasers at the bottom (say 5 to 10 pages per minute, where one page is A4 size) and the top (say 100 pages per minute, where one page is somewhat bigger or a different size). There are laser machines in the gap, mainly at the 20 pages per minute level, but the big marketing push is below this for the time being.

The 8 pages per minute laser printers based on the Canon engine and exemplified by the Hewlett-Packard LaserJet dominated the laser market in 1988, says Romtec, accounting for 81 per cent of unit sales. The latter half of the year saw the launch of the sub 1,000 Qume Crystalprint printing at 6 pages per minute and utilising Liquid Crystal Shutter technology. This is an area expected to grow significantly.

Laser is an abbreviation for 'light amplification by stimulated emission of radiation'. Unlike other forms of light, which spread in all directions, the laser is spatially coherent light which moves exclusively in a single direction

Laser is in fact an abbreviation for 'light amplification by stimulated emission of radiation'. Unlike other forms of light, which spread in all directions, the laser is spatially coherent light which moves exclusively in a single direction. Laser printers are also dubbed page printers, for obvious reasons. At the top end, while it cannot be denied that lasers are fast - very fast - and the quality they produce is very good, does the DP department (or MIS department) really need excellent quality printouts? It does of course depend on whose DP department they're in. For example, in a bank, where quality is desired, a laser printer will almost certainly be needed. By contrast, an inventory dump for an army's spare parts might well be able to use a cheaper printer.

To put matters into perspective, a 40 pages per minute laser printer operates at the equivalent of 2,000 lines per minute. To shell out for a good quality line matrix printer will set you back about 10,000 while a top end laser printer costs well over 100,000. The cost of ownership has also to be added in - for more about this, please turn to Chapter 6. Basically, you'll have to budget for 2p per copy, compared with 0.1p for a band printer.

In short, there's a lot of development work to be done on lasers before their price/performance figures come anywhere near to those offered by the established and proven line printers. Laser costs are declining (eg a model costing £2,500 in 1987 probably costs over £1,000 less these days), and laser manufacturers are tending to concentrate on developing the desktop rather than DP machines. But a really good machine will cost about £3,000.

As a cautionary note, it is best not to get swayed by low prices unless your application can stand it - if you spend £1,500 on a laser, plug it in and then expect it to churn out 5,000 copies a month, you'll be in for a shock. The £1,500 tag will probably mean it's a low end machine intended to get through a maximum of about 3,000 copies a month.

Limitations of Laser Printers

Most laser printers are restricted to A4 size paper only and colour is not seen as a core development. Furthermore, the units are not at all suited to multi-part forms, while label handling or envelope work can be problematic. If you've got an 8 to 12 page per minute machine, you're only going to have an output paper bin of about 200 sheets - and it is irritating if you are forever getting up to check the unit is loaded with paper. If you are lucky enough to have a £20,000 24 pages per minute machine, you will find that you have a 1,500 sheet output tray, which is extremely useful. Don't forget printers are expensive to buy and run, and you'll be lucky to get away without maintenance (*see* Chapter 7).

Advantages of Laser Printers

So much for the negative side of laser printers. They produce marvellous letter quality output, have many font options and produce good graphics. They are quiet and, for most applications, fast. They are easy to use (*see* Chapter 7), and their emulations (HP LaserJet or PostScript) are supported by leading software packages, and others with an eye to what is happening in the market. The latest machines feature dual paper hoppers - often one is used for plain paper and one for company headed letter paper.

Laser printers produce marvellous letter quality output, have many font options and produce good graphics. They are quiet and, for most applications, fast. They are easy to use and their emulations (HP LaserJet or PostScript) are supported by leading software packages

The resolution on these machines is 300 dots per inch, or much better than a NLQ matrix printer. But, although the quality is undeniably good, you can still see the dot structure of each printed character. Genicom is marketing a Canon engine based laser with a resolution of 400 x 400 dots per inch, which gives a superb output and offers a better throughput rate than most PostScript printers, due to its ACE page description language and raster image processor. The desktop publishing (DTP) market will gain even more from such resolution improvements, once the software drivers catch up.

For all those worried about unwelcome radiation emissions from laser machines, there are units which utilise light emitting diode arrays or liquid crystal shutter technology. With laser technology, a laser draws the image of the text or graphics on a light sensitive drum, to which the charged particles of toner are then attracted. Paper (the 'page') is run past the drum, whereupon it picks up the toner. A heating process fuses these together, the drum is cleared of toner and the process begins again.

With liquid crystal and light emitting diode technology, the principle is much the same. The laser is replaced and dots of light are aimed at a light sensitive drum. One area where they score is in their ability to handle A3 printing. They are also said to be more reliable. But lasers are better at graphics and offer more fonts.

> **LIGHT EMITTING DIODE (LED) AND LIQUID CRYSTAL SHUTTER (LCS) PRINTERS**
> These are the same as laser printers but use a different light source for the imaging process. In an LED printer the drum rotates below an array of light-emitting diodes, which flicker on and off to build up the image. In a liquid crystal printer a fluorescent light shines through a long narrow liquid crystal display, which flickers on and off to selectively block out the light from hitting the drum.

In other respects these printers work in exactly the same way as a laser printer, and have the same advantages and disadvantages. Mechanically the laser imaging system is more complex, so LED and crystal printers potentially have a cost advantage

INK JET, NON-IMPACT

> **INK JET PRINTERS**
> Ink jet printers fire ink directly on to paper without using a ribbon. The ink is usually shot from a vertical bank of nozzles, so characters are built up from a pattern of dots. Advantages are quietness and reasonably low cost. Output quality depends on the number of nozzles, but can be very high. Until recently, inkjets were fussy about the kind of paper they would print on, but the latest models have overcome this.

Ink jet technology is regarded as one of the most effective methods of printing, and can in fact be considered as non-impact matrix printing. As with matrix printers, ink jet units give you a choice between draft and NLQ modes. The technology uses only as much ink as is necessary to make an image, and has the flexibility to handle both text and graphics. Furthermore, it is being viewed as the best way to put colour on paper.

More than its fair share of problems have been dogging this technology until quite recently. Problems were primarily associated with the liquid ink technologies that were the only basis of ink jet printing. With liquid ink, print quality depends on the substrate, where the ink relied on evaporation or absorption into the paper to be able to dry. So the best print quality tended to be on poor paper, and poor print quality on high rag content quality bond, which is not an easy concept to market.

Large scale acceptance was therefore not likely to materialise. A major technical difficulty lay in the jets, which tended to clog up - there was a real dilemma in that the ink had to dry quickly on paper while it should not dry out in the printhead.

Solid ink technology is faster and quieter than daisywheel and dot matrix printing and can print text and graphics on virtually any medium

Solid ink technology may bring about a solution to this problem. This is a wax-based phase change material which is jetted at a higher temperature to harden on contact with the paper. Some ink locks into the paper's structure while the rest remains above the paper's surface to give well-defined and crisp characters. The high optical density yields strong blacks, while there is also a long shelf life and no deterioration of print quality with time. This technology is faster and quieter than daisywheel and dot matrix printing and can print text and graphics on virtually any medium (eg, tissue paper, overhead slide films and sandpaper). Ink jet printing provides more paper handling options and better print quality than a laser.

Ink from a pellet is melted and held in a reservoir in liquid form to be supplied to the ink jet mechanism. The ink remains liquid as long as the printer is on. Ink is drawn from the reservoir through a fill tube by capillary action and expelled through an orifice plate by the vibration of 32 corresponding piezoelectric crystals, which pump away piston fashion to disgorge the ink.

Consistent dot size and controlled dot placement give control over how the character is formed. Unlike the laser, where a complete page must be made up prior to printing, a serial printer does not have to compose a page prior to output.

Optimised logic seeking within a print line plus high speed vertical paper motion increases throughput significantly.

Weighing up against ink jet units is the simple fact that they have no track record on reliability, they have high costs of consumables and if you get hold of an early ink jet device, the chances are that you will need special paper and the quality of output may be below par.

Ink jet printers have speed ratings of anything from 30 characters per second to over 500 cps, ie similar to the matrix printers which fall into the £400 to £1,500 price band. But they score over the matrix machines in many ways, notably they are very quiet and have a good quality of text and graphics output.

THERMAL TRANSFER, NON-IMPACT

> **THERMAL TRANSFER PRINTERS**
> Melts dye from a special ribbon on to the paper. As with a matrix printer, characters are built up from a pattern of dots.

There are two main variants of this technique, for monochrome or colour use. The monochrome system uses a conventional-looking ribbon, held in a cassette much like an office typewriter. The colour printers use a sheet of film as wide as the page, passing three or four sheets of different colours over the page in succession to build up the image.

Mono thermal transfer printers give good results quietly, but are expensive to run. Colour thermal transfer printers again give excellent results, but are expensive both to buy and run.

Quality of output is indeed a byword with this technology, which is a non-impact matrix technology. The printed output is in fact said to be better than a laser, while the device itself is a lot quieter. Speeds of operation range from near 80 characters per second to about 300 characters per second. As with dot matrix printers, users can select draft or NLQ modes of printing.

These printers work through a character matrix of electrodes aiming dots of heat onto a thermal ribbon. This contains a special ink which melts onto the page to form a character out of the matrix of dots. The inked side of the ribbon is pressed into contact with the medium by the head and the heating elements in the head melt the ink and transfer it to the media, where it resolidifies. It is the number of the electrodes (between 9 and 40 thermo elements) and the ribbon quality which results in the very high quality. The 240 x 240 dots per inch capability allows the production of high resolution charts, diagrams and drawings. Besides a conventional black ribbon, a colour ribbon can be used. This is made up from consecutive segments of the primary colours, ie yellow, magenta and cyan. Each colour segment corresponds in length to the width of the print carriage, and each cycle of the primary colours is preceded by a short length of uninked ribbon. This transparent section is used by the printer to locate the individual colour bands.

Colour printing is achieved on a line-by-line basis, with the head traversing the line three times using each primary colour in turn, either on its own or in combination with the other primary colours. What can be produced in combination are yellow, magenta, cyan, red, green, blue and black. The background colour of the medium produces the eighth. Varying the dot density of each primary colour produces hundreds of different colours. And developments are proceeding all the time.

Although the cost of a thermal transfer unit - hovering around the £1,000 mark - makes it seem the bargain of the decade, you should look at the costs of ownership. Estimates can vary, but you should be prepared for 10p per page, because of the expensive ribbons and printhead. Also, if you're running a lot of letter quality work (and who wouldn't with this machine), you are going to require a sheet feeder to handle the cut sheets.

Although the cost of a thermal transfer unit - hovering around the £1,000 mark - makes it seem the bargain of the decade, you should look at the costs of ownership. Estimates can vary, but you should be prepared for 10p per page, because of the expensive ribbons and printhead

However, thermal transfer printing is good for A3 printing and for colour printing. You can get units with single and double drawer sheet feed, plus an envelope feed which then lends the unit to letters and mailshots. Multiple fonts and graphics further enhance these attributes. However, the cost of coloured thermal paper can be quite substantial.

MAGNETOGRAPHIC, NON-IMPACT

MAGNETOGRAPHIC PRINTING PROCESS
The magnetographic printing process consists of writing magnetically the page to be printed on a rotating drum, toning the latent image on the drum with magnetic ink, transferring the image to paper and finally fixing the printed image using low heat. People claim its advantage is that it uses tried and tested technology, and is simple in design and manufacture.

Typical operating speeds are 90 pages per minute, equivalent to 6,000 lines per minute at 8 lines per inch. In addition, these engines will allow you to print reports in a condensed font and, by rotating the data, you can print two forms side-by-side on one page, effectively reducing the print run by 50 per cent.

It is also possible to mix character fonts within a line, change spacing between lines, rotate the page through 0, 90, 180 and 270 degrees, print in reverse video, underscore, highlight characters or words within a page and print proportional characters within a line.

You can't of course run multi-part stationery through these machines, but at these speeds who would need to? It also doesn't handle colour.

One interesting feature is a software program which runs on an industry standard PC-XT, AT or compatible. The programme allows logos and overlays to be created in data form, which are stored on floppy disk. The printer merges the live data from the system with the data stored on the floppy disk to produce pages containing the composite images. This allows the printer to be used to print business forms together with the data that goes on them. Preprinted stationery becomes a thing of the past.

A software programme is available which allows logos to be created in data form, which are stored on floppy disk. The printer merges live data with this data to produce business forms. Preprinted stationary therefore becomes a thing of the past

A high resolution is derived from a 240 by 240 dots per inch matrix. A power stacker is mandatory to remove the printouts as fast as possible and interfaces are usually IBM 3203-5 emulation.

ION DEPOSITION, NON-IMPACT

> **ION DEPOSITION PRINTERS**
> Like the laser printer, this is part of the page printer group. The operating sequence is identical for all page printers; only the way in which the character pattern is produced on the drum is different.

With an ion deposition or ionic printer, an ionic cartridge extends over the whole width of the aluminium oxide print drum and is used as the exposure element. Digital information transmitted to the ionic cartridge controls the shooting of ions onto the rotating surface of the print drum. The positioning of the hole pattern allows a print resolution of 300 dots per inch. Ion deposition printers are known to be more frugal with their toners than other non-impact printers. Their costs are high, however, so high usage levels are required to obtain the best out of them. The machines are rugged and reliable.

CHAPTER 2

BUYING A PRINTER

HORSES FOR COURSES

Buying a printer for a computer system is not a straightforward task. The same amount of thought and effort that is applied to evaluating what computer system to buy in the first place needs to be applied to that part of the configuration that can never be reduced in size - the printer. The number of mechanical parts can be reduced to the bare minimum, but the size of paper we all read from will not reduce - therefore the printer will not shrink below a defined size.

DUTY CYCLES

Two key considerations are duty cycles (ie the sort of work a printer will do - see below for more details), and cost efficiency.

In duty cycles, the amount of time a printer will be in action is analysed, together with the type of application and workload. To take an absurd example, it would be no good buying a cheap printer from a High Street outlet if your application required overnight unattended print runs. Likewise it would be no use buying an exotic high speed laser printer if all you wanted to do was print out a cash flow forecast twice a week, requiring 20 minutes use of the printer.

> In duty cycles, the amount of time a printer will be in action is analysed, together with the type of application and workload

The term duty cycle refers to the actual number of lines printed per printer divided by the maximum possible for that printer at 100 per cent character density, which is the number of lines printed per page times the number of characters printed per line. Total duty cycle is then determined by

BUYING A PRINTER 23

multiplying duty cycle by character density. Take the example of a Dataproducts band printer which is a 600 lines per minute 132 column unit actually printing at 180 lines per minute. This gives a duty cycle of 30 per cent. But if only 79 characters per line are printed (60 per cent) and 34 lines are printed per standard fanfold page (40 per cent), the character density is 24 per cent. Total duty is now 7.2 per cent.

Duty cycle and character density have a significant impact on mean time before failure (MTBF) - take the example where MTBF is approximately 1,100 hours or over 90 weeks (five day, 40 hour working). As duty cycle and character density increase, MTBF is reduced considerably. At 12 hours per day, 60 per cent duty cycle and 60 per cent character density, MTBF is 650 hours or 53 weeks.

So on a heavy total duty cycle application environment, it can be more cost effective to purchase multiple, cheaper printers, eg two 600 lines per minute printer instead of one 1,200 lines per minute unit.

Apart from MTBF calculations, the mean time between service calls (MTBSC) figure is a vital factor, in particular for the printer user. Repair and maintenance costs are increasing (*see* Chapter 7) and the demands are quite simply that a MTBSC figure is obtained and adhered to.

If a high speed high reliability printer is purchased and operated at low duty cycles, the MTBSC is extended. But conversely, if the same printer is operated beyond its intended workload, the MTBSC is dramatically decreased, as well as the cost of ownership. Here, a printer manufacturer would recommend upgrading to a higher capacity printer.

You should also seek a guarantee for the mean time to repair (MTTR) figure.

Duty Cycle Advice

As a useful tip, watch out for what a manufacturer, dealer or distributor tells you if you ask 'What is the duty cycle for the printer I'm going to buy?' Some will happily quote their machine's MTTF figure (the mean time to failure) - and it will be impressive. But check whether they are referring to power on hours or working hours, because the two vary enormously.

As a rule, duty cycles these days tend to be 25 per cent and downwards, and band printers, for example, will be designed around a duty cycle of 25 per cent. Laser printers will have duty cycles of 5 per cent.

COST EFFICIENCY

It should be remembered that cost is not the only guiding factor in printing technology. The question of cost efficiency is very often calculated on the basis of the cost per printed page. This figure will be provided (or should be provided) by the particular printer manufacturer.

However, as well as a cost calculation, you will have to take other variables into account too. Take the example of someone moving into the desktop publishing area, who wants to create and print documents with various typefaces, graphics and photographs, but doesn't know whether it will be possible to print it at all. Indeed, it will not be possible on some laser printers, and even if this can be achieved on others, the cost of extras, components, software and disruption will be high.

In this case, a person will also have to consider how much time and resources will be consumed getting certain of the more ambitious tasks out of the way. Prudent advice is that it might

BUYING A PRINTER 25

be worth subcontracting the more demanding tasks to specialist outside suppliers.

Operating Costs

The costs associated with operating a printer will be calculated from the unit's use of consumables like paper and toners (if you're running a laser machine), as well as allowances for space costs, plus those costs incurred when you have to exchange worn parts. The costs of power, paper, ribbons, ink pellets or cartridges, and toner will depend on your printing volume and are consequently variable. Therefore, they can be difficult to assess.

Maintenance Contracts

To these definite costs you have to add the cost of a maintenance contract, because, like it or not, the bets are that you are going to need to call out an engineer at some time in the lifetime of your printer (*see* Chapter 7).

To operating costs you have to add the cost of a maintenance contract, because at some stage you are going to need to call out an engineer for your printer

Note particularly that the intervals recommended by the manufacturer for fitting ribbons, exchanging toner kits, print drums, developer kits, fixer units, daisywheels, etc, must be followed. If a fault does occur during the guarantee period, you ought to be aware whether it is the manufacturer or the dealer who is responsible for the handling of claims under guarantee - and for how long it is covered. Generally speaking, the working life of individual components has to be considered too.

If a fault can only be repaired in the workshop, it is important to know who will do this and how long the repair is likely to take. You should then also check whether a replacement printer will be made available.

The Real Cost of Owning a Printer

So, having got this far, how do you work out the real cost of owning a printer? It may sound obvious, but you have to amortise the costs over the total life of the printer, and you will have to anticipate the number of pages that are to be produced per month.

You will need to add the costs of accessories per month (*see* Chapter 6). For a laser printer this will include all the necessary storage space costs and payments for software such as page description languages, font generators and additional character sets. For thermal transfer printers, it's the costs of special ribbons and printheads, etc.

You will need to add the spare parts costs per month. Then you will need to add the costs of consumables - such as paper - divided by the number of pages produced per month.

Before you choose your printer, you should have some idea of how much printing you will do each month

But before you choose your printer it must be stressed that you should have some idea of how much printing you will do each month. Not only this, but you will have to estimate how this will increase in the future (remember, the mere presence of a good printer will tend to boost the volume of throughput). So a thoughtful calculation will prove to you that buying a more productive and efficient machine will turn out more economical in both short and long terms.

One bit of advice at this point though - remember that there is no 'number one' printer on the market. The ideal does not exist, for the simple reason that your needs are going to be different from those of the person down the road. When you are choosing your printer, it makes sound sense to read the technical/trade press, particularly when printer surveys and performance analyses are published. They will usually provide the most up-to-date information.

It would be prudent for you to have a clear set of objectives properly matched to your needs and budget. It is also advisable to be sure of the print quality required.

Whether it be from laser, thermal transfer, dot matrix or whatever technology, a resolution of 240 dots per inch produces good characters. At 400 dots per inch, printed text compares well with typeset copy, and higher resolutions are really only necessary for the highest quality of text production, grey scale levels in graphics and for plate making.

WHAT TO LOOK FOR IN PAGE PRINTING

The advent of the cheap 'page printer' quickened the pulse of many an office manager and spurred them to thoughts of a future with no necessity to stock pre-printed forms, and no delays in proofing amendments to sales and pricing literature. They even began to look at the prospect of 'in house' publishing for the smaller quantity runs which would otherwise require typesetting outside the office.

Many page printers address the more basic needs of wordprocessing, emulating as they do such daisywheel products as the Diablo 630. They do provide some flexibility in the number of typefaces which may be combined in a single page of text. This is usually one or two resident fonts, with optional plug-in modules. To exploit font flexibility, something more than the simpler wordprocessing programs used with daisywheel printers is required (*see* Chapter 4). Likewise, the screen resolution should be such as will permit reasonable portrayal of the character styles in use.

One can piece together systems using bold and inverse text to achieve a fair visual aid to page layout, but the printed results will leave a lot to be desired and require rework. For efficiency, you are going to need a front end that's equipped with a little more sophistication in order to handle, say, three or more typestyles to a page. True, it's going to cost, but do bear in mind the foregoing advice.

Any system required to churn out multiple copies of lengthy reports, price lists, etc, is unlikely to use one of the cheaper laser printers. Some printers, for example, are marketed as being suitable for 3,000 pages a month - at a print speed of, say, seven pages per minute - which amounts to a running time of 20 minutes a day. The material costs associated with several of the similarly-priced page printers would, on examination, also preclude them from higher duty cycles.

OPC-Based Page Printers

The cheaper page printers are mainly, but not exclusively, based on the use of a low-cost, non-toxic imaging surface referred to as OPC (short for organic photoconductor). In contrast to the conventional selenium imaging surface used in higher throughput copiers, with surface life of up to 100,000 pages, OPC lasts from 4,000 to 20,000 pages. However, being non-toxic, it is user replaceable.

The cheaper page printers are mainly based on the use of a low-cost, non-toxic imaging surface referred to as OPC (organic photoconductors)

With Canon engines, it is discarded along with the fusing system, whenever the toner supply is exhausted, whereas in most other OPC-based machines, it is a separately-serviced component. This design philosophy of replaceable short life cycle components has resulted in very low-priced products with high costs of ownership and (in some cases) machine life-cycles of only 100,000 pages.

Other Page Printing Technologies

In stark contrast to the OPC-based machines, there is a magnetic drum in a Bull printer which has a life cycle of 10 million pages and prints on fan-fold paper at 90 pages per minute. The throughput is rated at 750,000 pages per month, with claims of rates as high as 500 pages per minute.

The majority of in-house and multi-user publishing systems are expected to lie in the band of 5,000 to 20,000 pages per month of printed throughput. All these make full use of font flexibility, text rotation and graphics. Printing rates go up to 20 pages per minute and life cycles reach one million pages (or better).

Systems servicing this need include the light emitting diode (LED) imaging array driven laser type machine which has a resolution of 400 dots per inch and throughput printing rate of 18 pages per minute. You can also get an LED array type machine with a user replaceable OPC imaging surface which prints at 12 pages per minute with a resolution of 240 dots per inch and a quoted duty cycle of 12,000 pages per month.

There are other machines - eg from Xerox, Fujitsu, Mita, Ricoh and Philips, etc - which meet or exceed this duty cycle.

There is also a page printer which utilises magnetic imaging technology to print at a rate of 10 pages per minute with a resolution of 240 dots per inch. Unlike other low-priced printers, this unit is a high-duty cycle machine with low unit costs per printed page. A further point is that magnetic imaging results in the image being retained on the drum until erased, unlike laser technology which must refresh the image for every print cycle.

Magnetic imaging results in the image being retained on the drum until erased, unlike laser technology which must refresh the image for every print cycle - this enables the printer to be run at 30 pages per minute in a repeat mode

This latter feature enables the printer to be run at 30 pages per minute in a repeat mode, which places its average throughput rate well above its basic 10 pages per minute. So in the case of even modest publishing runs, this one would outstrip those costing three to four times more.

But you have to take into account many variables too, not least continuity of supplier, spare parts and consumables, what the dealer is like, etc. You must be exhaustive in your search.

BUYING A LASER PRINTER

Having studied the latest literature, technical specfications, and scanned the technical press, you be getting some idea of what you want. When considering which type to get, remember that by 1992 page printers are expected to account for nearly 55 per cent of the printer market in Europe. This represents a rate of increase of over 35 per cent per year.

By 1992, page printers are expected to account for nearly 55 per cent of the printer market in Europe

First, take the price of the basic model, plus the costs of any possible memory expansion, and toner, print drum, developer and fixer unit consumables. Look for a printing speed generally of at least 10 pages per minute (but *see* Chapter 4) and internal memory of at least 512 kB. Look for memory expansion possibilities to at least 1.5 MB.

The life of the printer should be at least 300,000 pages and the life of the drum should be optimally 10,000 sheets. You should aim for a toner consumption of roughly one cartridge per 3,000 pages.

When you switch the machine on, check what sort of a warm up period you're going to get. As a guide, a minute is the limit you should aim for. If you're worried about noise, check the noise level on standby and the noise level during operation. These ought to be about 45 dBA on standby (maximum) and 55 dBA during operation (maximum).

With sound, the hertz (Hz) rating measures the tone of the sound; the decibel (dB) rating measures the intensity of sound. You'll start to hear whispers at about 5 dB. It's when the level reaches 76 dB that you begin to find sounds irritating - this level corresponds to heavy traffic.

Check the interface (*see* Chapter 3). Is the unit designed to connect (quickly) with a range of desk top personal computers, multi-user or networked systems, for example. Does it offer a built-in parallel interface and RS232/RS422 serial interface, Centronics, AppleTalk, etc.

You will need to look at the fonts that are provided as standard. What extras are there? Your printer's resolution these days should be at least 300 x 300 dots per inch to give good quality output.

32 PROFITING FROM YOUR PRINTER

Check that variation of typeface parameters (eg, point size) is possible, and that additional typefaces can be loaded, plus forms, logos and signatures. The point size you should look for should be at least 8 to 14 points, with a pitch of 10 to 20 characters per inch for variety. As well as being able to print in portrait and landscape format, your printer should possess a number of printer emulations (eg, Hewlett-Packard, IBM Graphics, Epson, Diablo, Apple).

For desktop publishing work you'll need an internal page description language such as PostScript (*see* Chapter 4). And you'll need a clearly written manual from the supplier too.

On paper, go for the largest paper cartridges and stackers or trays that you can lay your hands on - these days it's the 250 sheet trays that are in demand, although even this is not necessarily enough. Check if additional cartridges are possible and whether a collating device can be connected. Some machines on the market offer the facility of a selection of paper stacking method (ie face up or face down), easily switchable.

> On paper, go for the largest paper cartridges and stackers or trays that you can lay your hands on. Check if additional cartridges are possible, and whether a collating device can be connected

Check the weight of paper you can safely go up to - some machines will allow you to run with 140 gsm (grams per square metre) for example. Others will not. Also see if the printer will accept foil, labels and envelopes. For more illumination on this topic, *see* Chapter 5.

Look to see if you can understand the front panel. If you have to spend ages poring over the manual, and you still can't get it right - look elsewhere. The two go hand-in-hand really. You must have a clearly-written manual to tell you what to do and you must have a comprehensible front panel to know what the manual contains.

The cost per printed page target, if you've got all your calculations right, should work out at 5p maximum. Get below this and you are doing very well.

BUYING A BAND PRINTER

When selecting a band printer, it is essential that the choice is made not only on the basis of speed but also on the ability of the unit to operate within the application duty cycle.

MEASURING PERFORMANCE

Once you've done all the calculations you're going to do, and worked out the full costings, how can you be sure you've chosen a printer which best suits your needs - when the performance of one is measured in characters per second and that of another is in pages per minute? To complicate things further, a description follows of a particular standard set of performance measurements which, it is claimed, would end all such confusion.

There were until recently several ways to measure the performance of computer printers. Some were formalised, such as the DIN standard letter while some have simply become accepted over the years - such as the characters per second (CPS) rating for daisywheel and matrix printers and, more recently, the pages per minute (PPM) rating for laser printers.

Unfortunately for the user, however, a great deal of licence has been taken with these figures by some manufacturers and these informal tests no longer provide any reliable measure of

34 PROFITING FROM YOUR PRINTER

performance. For example, some manufacturers quote CPS ratings based on a burst speed over only a small portion of a total line; or speeds that can only be achieved if the printer is printing text in a small typeface rather than the accepted 10 or 12 characters per inch (CPI). Indeed the usual default pitch on any printer is taken as 10 CPI. So inevitably the publication of such unreliable figures has lead to increasing confusion among users.

A similar problem exists with ratings for the speed of laser printers. In most cases, speeds for these units are quoted in pages per minute (PPM), but the published statistics are seldom met in the real world when printing from normal applications software. A particular problem is the delay between the initiation of the print command from the host computer and the appearance of the first sheet from the printer.

European Printer Performance

Several key European computer and computer printer manufacturers have got together to agree a common set of standard tests which attempt to compare printers regardless of the technology they use, taking full account of all factors. Known as the European Printer Performance Tests (EPPTs), the set is an attempt to introduce rational measurements into what was otherwise fast becoming an irrational situation.

> Several key European computer and computer printer manufacturers have got together to agree a set of standard tests which attempt to compare printers regardless of the technology they use - this is known as the European Printer Performance Tests

The group includes Bull, Facit, Hermes Precisa, Nixdorf, Newbury Data Recording, Olivetti, Philips and Wenger. The group set out to devise a sound method for measuring the throughput of a printer rather than any measure of speed.

While there has been, and is continuing to be, resistance from the Japanese manufacturers to the EPPTs, the tests have been accepted by ECMA (European Computer Manufacturers Association) as one of its standards. Meanwhile the group of nine is continuing in discussions with ISO (International Standards Organisation) and DIN (German standards body) for formal acceptance of EPPT specifications as both European and International Standards.

It must be stressed that the tests are intended for application at the systems end of the computer printer spectrum and not the personal computer or High Street end. Outside the UK the concept of the EPPTs standard is much better appreciated. The French in particular are known for their particularly aggressive attitude towards Japanese marketing practices.

While the EPPTs are not in anyway ideal, they are the only tool available that has addressed the problem of the over-enthusiastic claims made by people of many nationalities.

Performance Testing

The EPPT specification of pages per hour (PPH) is a realistic test designed to simulate a typical group of user applications, printed in accordance with well defined parameters. The three tests of text processing, spreadsheet and graphics are fairly common output for many business users these days.

Performance testing simulates the real user application of printing a relatively short document. In this mode the printer is expected to operate at full speed, and the results obtained are a true representation of throughput on short duration

36 PROFITING FROM YOUR PRINTER

print jobs. In particular, this test highlights any delays there may be prior to printing the first page.

With endurance testing, the printer is subjected to a one hour continuous trial. While perhaps not a typical environment for an office or desktop printer, it is included to highlight any printer slowdown effects caused by dot density limitations or adverse temperature rises.

It should be stressed that the EPPTs exist only to measure a printer's throughput performance and not to evaluate any other printer feature such as character shaping, paper handling, colour reproduction, etc. The specification defines the minimum level of testing and includes print tests with both single sheets and the maximum part set the printer has been designed to handle, if this is three parts or greater. Where different results are achieved with these tests, the two are shown side-by-side in the resulting tabular report.

For **text processing**, the EPPTs use the standard DIN 32751 letter, which includes European diacritic characters such as 'u' and 'o', at a standard 10 CPI and six lines per inch.

As standard, the **spreadsheet test** pattern is set at 132 column line length, six lines per inch, in draft quality. Printers with a line length of only 80 columns are tested at 17.1 CPI in place of the normal 10 CPI.

The **graphics test** comprises a histogram printed at two resolutions: low graphics at 60 x 72 dots per inch (DPI); and high resolution at a minimum 120 x 145 DPI. Such tests are not applicable to daisywheel printers but the essential point of them is that manufacturers are prohibited from using text characters and block graphics to beat the standard. The only commands allowed in fact are line feed, carriage return, form feed, line feed distance setting and graphics execution.

Neither alphanumeric, block graphics nor space characters can be used to print a chart.

The dimension and position on the page of the graphics image are tightly defined with a height of 127 mm and a width of 165.1 mm, the width of one column being specified at 25.4 mm. The height of the four columns must be 25.4, 50.8, 76.2 and 101.6 mm and the space between each column is specified at 12.7 mm. Any deviation to the standard is permitted only if the printer has difficulties printing the image exactly to specification, in which case it shall produce a test image larger, and never smaller, than that specified.

The objective of the EPPT was 'to set several features permitting a comprehensive evaluation of printer performance.' The manufacturers set out to design tests to suit all printer types and capabilities and to specify the manner in which test data should be presented. The consortium claims that for the first-time buyers can truly compare like-for-like data presented in a consistent pattern.

> The objective of the EPPT was 'to set features permitting a comprehensive evaluation of printer performance'

Printers can be tested in both draft and best quality mode and the results separately shown. Because the perception of print quality is subjective, test results must also be interpreted and recorded to include details of the virtual matrix of the printer - the highest possible character definition offered - specified in DPI both vertically and horizontally.

The Japanese printer manufacturers claim that if the EPPT specification of pages per hour is enforced - as a brick in the wall of fortress Europe 1992 for example - there really is no discernible difference from, say, the existing characters per second results.

The scenario to compare it all with, say the Japanese, is the petrol changeover from gallons to litres, vis-a-vis car manufacturers and petrol stations. Stickers appeared bearing direct comparisons between what everyone was used to - pricing per gallon - and the new standard - pricing per litre. Similarly, manufacturers would quote in litres per hour and miles per hour equivalents. So you can now imagine your printer resplendent with stickers declaring its speed of operation in characters per second and pages per hour equivalent.

PITFALLS IN COMPARING DIFFERENT PRINTERS

It is difficult, however, for a dot matrix printer which transfers data line-by-line to be equated with a printer which prints in pages per minute. For pages per hour measurement, a cut sheet feeder is required. If there is high speed paper feed, ie continuous paper, then there is an automatic jump to the next page, which then makes the particular printer faster than a single sheet fed printer.

Laser printers are equipped with at least one sheet feeder as standard; matrix printers are not. Indeed sheet feeders are options on many other types too. Many believe the pages per hour argument is the wrong way to approach dot matrix technology, except perhaps where a mail merge operation of about 60 letters is being handled.

A key difference indeed between different printer technologies is whether a particular technology is suited to handling single or cut sheets, or continuous stationery

A key difference indeed between different printer technologies is whether a particular technology is suited to handling single or cut sheets, or continuous stationery. Lasers are intended to work with cut sheets, and they come equipped with paper trays that remind you of the photocopier. But they're no good for printing on to continuous stationery.

Non-laser printers are fitted with a platen of the type found on typewriters, which allow you to feed in cut sheets - manually, one at a time. But they're no good for feeding in multiple sheets. For this privilege, you'll have to shell out a lot of money, way over the cost of the printer itself. And this is practically mandatory for letters and the like which will necessitate printing on to cut sheets. The problems don't end there either, because you'll undoubtedly have to get software to drive these optional sheet feeders - so, the advice is, talk to someone about the unreliability factors of these units.

As usual, time will see what results are brought out of the arguments. But certainly there would be red faces all round in those staunchly European companies whose badged-up printers were originally manufactured in the Far East, who found they'd broken their own rules and even their own laws.

Meanwhile, having had its specifications nominally accepted by the European Computer Manufacturers Association, the EPPT group of manufacturers now awaits further acknowledgements from the ISO and DIN organisations.

CHAPTER 3

CONNECTING A PRINTER TO YOUR SYSTEM

Once a computer is installed, how do you connect it to the printer? All sorts of terms like serial and parallel interfaces, V24/RS232 and Centronics extension cables, PC and IEEE cables, twinax and coax connectors, etc, etc, begin to manifest themselves. How do you use different peripherals like dot matrix printers, letter quality printers, line boosters, plotters and modems together, particularly if both serial and parallel interfaces are involved.

Connecting up remotely-sited printers can be a problem, depending on the distance. Other problems can stem from the time taken by a computer to dump files to a slow peripheral, so the area of buffering is scrutinised. A further area is sharing a printer between computers, to save the cost of unnecessary peripherals, make fuller use of existing hardware and avoid reconnection time by using different types of switching.

IBM CONNECTIVITY AND SYSTEMS CONNECTION

IBM users have encountered difficulties due to the non-uniformity of its computers, software and interfaces across its entire ranges. With its printers, for example, coaxial cabling is used to connect devices to the 370 series, 303X, 308X, 4300 and 309X mainframes, and 37XX front end processors. Twinax cabling is used to connect printers to System/3X and AS/400 minis.

Connecting up IBM PCs is a different matter. Users normally have to grapple with the intricacies of parallel interface ports and metal shielded cabling, or serial RS232C linkages. The PC end of the market does not have a major requirement for coax/twinax.

CONNECTING A PRINTER TO YOUR SYSTEM

Until now, the DP department/MIS scenario has been one where an IBM mainframe or mini is directly linked via a coax or twinax cable to a systems printer. A line from the same mainframe or mini could connect up with dedicated terminals or PCs through an interface board.

If the DP/MIS department is using a non-systems printer, there is a need for protocol conversion between the printer and the incoming coax or twinax line. This is generally a messy external box solution, but it does work.

There is now a discernible move to a neater and cleaner environment, an internal solution. It is possible to use a flexible resource that is not as expensive as a regular dedicated system printer.

Protocol converters offer the user an internal interface with external boxes. People involved in selling and fitting protocol converters rarely offer a total package of printer and interface. They sell protocol converters. Printer manufacturers will sell printers. It is rare indeed for a PC printer manufacturer to offer system printers and even rarer to offer, as a separate product, the coax and twinax interface board for use with existing printers. The most common internal PC solution for linking PCs into IBM mainframes has been the IRMA card, which any systems user will instantly recognise.

Offering the internal twinax/coax interface for IBM environments provides advantages in connectivity, technology, reliability and availability

Offering the internal twinax/coax interface for IBM environments, as on Epson systems printers, provides advantages in the key areas of connectivity, technology, reliability and availability, the range of products, hardware support and good documentation.

Typical market areas that should be interested in this innovation are all IBM mini and mainframe sites which need reliable, flexible and cost-effective solutions to their printing needs.

As an example, consider the head offices of a large (imaginary) corporation. With the company's 3090 mainframe, the 3X74 controllers are rarely fully-populated. The company's PS/2 network is attached, as are terminals and PCs with IRMA cards. Dedicated systems printers are there as well, plus a System/38, linked in from offices in another building.

The systems manager is running a pilot application for which he connects a 400 characters per second (cps) systems printer through the 3X74 controller. The coax cable provides the direct link. The System/38 manager drops by and sees the work. 'Any chance of my using that model printer on my system?' he asks. 'Not unless you are coax,' comes the reply. 'Doesn't it handle twinax?' 'No, this printer is for mainframe use only and cannot be used with your mini.'

The network manager also drops by and says, 'That model printer would also suit my department down to the ground.' She likes the price/performance statistics the printer offers, and is considering it as a high volume terminal printer on her LAN (local area network) servers. But her kit is not coax either.

In this example, what is required is a flexible printing resource, that is not as expensive as regular dedicated system printers.

The IBM Computer Users Association believes that 'any improvement in connectivity is always extremely welcome. One of the problems in connectivity has always been in the printer area. The facility to address printers across different communications media is most welcome indeed.'

CONNECTING A PRINTER TO YOUR SYSTEM 45

General industry comments from a variety of sources all agree that the development is a good idea. The consensus is that there is a need for a wider variety of interfaces to printers.

The industry consensus is that there is a need for a wider variety of interfaces to printers

A problem of buying IBM has been that most of the PC products do not attach to twinax/coax standards, and most of the DP products do not attach to PC standards.

PARALLEL OR SERIAL COMMUNICATIONS?

When connecting the printer to a (personal) computer, you have to determine whether a parallel or serial connection should be used. Indeed many computers only provide one type of connection for a printer. But if both types of connection are available on the computer, it is normally better to use the parallel interface for the printer, leaving the serial port free for devices such as modems.

If you are in any doubt about which type of connection to make, or cannot find the reference in your computer manual, consult your printer/computer dealer.

All text and programs used by your computer are stored as electrical signals which represent binary numbers. These electrical signals are switched on to represent a binary '1' digit, or off to represent a '0' digit.

Binary digits are stored in groups of eight, giving the capability of representing any number in the range 0 to 255. A grouping of eight binary digits or bits is known as a byte.

One byte has to be sent for each character of text whenever data is transferred. Bytes can be transmitted simultaneously (ie, in parallel) using eight separate wires or one at a time (ie, serial) down a single wire.

Parallel communication is a simple operation from the user's point of view because there are wires available with which the printer can be controlled by the computer. The printer can tell the computer when it is ready to receive more data. Furthermore, no speed of transmission factor has to be specified and nor do any of the many other settings required for serial communication. The advantage of serial data transfer is that much simpler hardware can be used, with many fewer wires.

All text and programs used by your computer are stored as electrical signals which represent binary numbers. These electrical signals are switched on to represent a binary '1' digit, or off to represent a binary '0'

The disadvantage of serial data transfer is that data has to be sent and received in a much more complicated way. A stream of characters cannot simply be sent as a continuous sequence of binary digits, as it would be very difficult to tell where one character finished and the next began.

Likewise, the printer must know at what rate it is expecting data to be sent, and it must receive that data in recognisable packages. Finally, there is the problem that the printer is unable to process the data as fast as it is received. This means that there has to be a system for indicating that no more data can be received. The different settings which must agree between the computer and printer form the communications protocol.

CONNECTING A PRINTER TO YOUR SYSTEM 47

COMMUNICATING WITH YOUR COMPUTER

An interface allows a computer and a printer to be linked together with a cable. Whatever you do, however, don't fall into the trap of assuming that all printers will work properly with your computer. To get a really good result, the hardware and software have to be fully compatible. This is a key issue.

Your printer must have the same interface as your computer. This is what is meant by hardware compatibility. Your printer should furthermore accept industry standard codes and the codes used in the software package you are running. This is what is meant by software compatibility.

Your printer must have the same interface as your computer. This is what is meant by hardware compatibility

So to get your printer to print, you must check that the interface on your computer is the same as the one on your printer.

Deciding on which interface to use for your computer is really quite simple. If you are at all unsure about which interface your computer has, first have a look through your computer manual. Whatever you do, do not rely on examining the connector at the back of your computer - the parallel interface connector on IBM and compatible option boards is of the same type as the serial connector on many other types of computer.

Some computers have other types of interface. For example, some computers have an IEEE-488 interface or a buffer interface where the buffer is large (32 to 128 KB), or a serial interface where the equipment requires a current loop connection. Generally these do not add features not already available using built-in interfaces. Furthermore, some of these will no longer be available and others will not be available in all countries.

The IEEE-488 system allows a user to connect computers, printers, disk drives and many types of other data-handling equipment so that they can share data freely. Manufacturers may offer two types of IEEE-488 interface to allow connection of their printers to such a network. A basic ability to operate in the IEEE-488 address and listen-only modes is one option. The other is to have a data buffer and a line monitor function, to provide a diagnostic printout of IEEE-488 commands received through the interface.

Buffer interfaces can be installed to free the computer more quickly for other tasks, if you often find yourself turning out large quantities of text and your software does not have a background printing facility to allow you to carry on working. Serial and parallel buffer interfaces are marketed to increase a printer's data buffering capacity and can be 32 or 128 KB (say, 10 to 40 pages) in size.

An interface that conforms to the Current Loop standard rather than RS-232C requires the installation of an optional interface. What you should look for in a serial interface are: a wide range of baud rates, a choice of 7 bit or 8 bit data and support for Current Loop operation in addition to RS-232C.

Furthermore, other desirable features are XON/XOFF protocol (a system in which the printer transmits a signal to the computer to indicate that it cannot accept more data, and a second signal when it is once more ready), a loopback self-test mode (which allows direct testing of the functions of the interface without connecting a computer), and a disable switch (interfaces with a disable switch can be left installed while the parallel interface is being used, but only one interface should be connected at a time).

CONNECTING A PRINTER TO YOUR SYSTEM

The Apple II, II+ and IIe computers do not have a printer interface as a standard feature. Parallel interface boards are available for the Apple which have software to control the functions of the printer, taking account of the particular requirements of the Apple operating system and the way software has been written. Units marketed control only the basic functions of a printer, or support graphics facilities and other commands required for some software.

> Ideally you should be able to use a different interface at any time, but you should connect up only one of your printer's interfaces at any one time

Ideally you should be able to use a different interface at any time, but you should connect up only one of your printer's interfaces at any one time.

EMULATIONS

As interfaces are to hardware compatibility between printers and computers, so emulations are to software compatibility. The software you're running on your system sends data to the printer in particular formats using defined codes. The key as to whether or not your printer will be compatible with the software you want so desperately to use is whether it can understand the format that is being sent to you.

To put this plainly, an emulation will enable a printer to mimic another printer so it can interpret the standard printer codes which are being squirted at it. Most of the software marketed these days will support a great number of printers, but you might be unlucky and be using a machine that doesn't appear on any of the supported lists that accompany most leading software packages. Be assured, however, that most printers are supplied with a few different emulations. These will be based on the ones most certain to be supported by most software packages.

Examples are: with daisywheels it's the Diablo 630 standard; with 9-pin matrix it's Epson FX series, IBM Proprinters or IBM's Epson manufactured Graphics Printer; for 24-pin matrix it's Epson LQ series; with lasers it's Hewlett-Packard LaserJet series (although Canon does all the leg work on the hardware and supplies most consumables); in the high end of printer ranges, interfaces can get a trifle muddied but IBM predominates if only by dint of market share.

Some words of caution are now called for. Emulations are not guaranteed to work that well. Imagine finding that what you have printed out on one printer will not dump on another that's ostensibly offering the same emulation.

Part of the problem derives from the fact that daisywheel printers (for example) have standard emulations that have been around for a number of years. Emulations are based on raw, basic printers so by mimicking them you won't be able to make use of any extra features that your printer may be able to provide.

Laser printers are much more sophiscated than a matrix printer could ever be and their standard emulation is consequently much more up-to-date

A lot of difficulties are overcome with laser printers. They're much more sophisticated than, say, a matrix printer could ever be and their standard emulation is consequently much more up-to-date. Furthermore there's the page description language PostScript, a feature to be found on the high-end laser printers - any software that offers PostScript can work with any PostScript printer. No performance restrictions are imposed either, unlike with emulations.

The main purpose of PostScript is to give the user more control over moving around the elements that are used to make up a page. A good example of this is easy scaling up of fonts to whatever size and a lot of impressive shading work, plus interesting graphics effects. These printers are, however, slower than non-PostScript printers and they cost up to an extra 1,000 for these additional features.

PRINTER DRIVERS

Software manufacturers have come up with a new device called prinnter drivers. Compatibility problems are therefore being seen to occur more in printer drivers than emulations, which are increasingly being viewed as holding back the sophisticated features that today's printers boast.

This is an area you might like to think about carefully. The software manufacturers are now supplying software with many printer drivers incorporated.

A PERSONAL EXAMPLE

To prepare the typescript for this book, I used the wordprocessing package MultiMate Advantage II from Ashton-Tate, running on an IBM PS/2 Model 50 Z. The printer I used mostly was an Epson LQ-1050, but there were also times when a Qume Crystal Print, Dataproducts 8022 and Fujitsu DL3300 were attached. The only problems experienced were to do with paper jams and crumbly sprocket holes in the fanfold stationery. The printers themselves were fine and did their jobs.

The point of this example is to demonstrate what Ashton-Tate has done with MultiMate Advantage II. The company has added a Printer Enhancement Pack (PEP), a software package offering a range of new features and enhancements, especially for laser printing.

After a series of screen prompts, PEP can be installed quickly. During installation, you are asked what printer is to be used. If a laser printer is selected, PEP displays a list of available cartridges (including soft fonts and cartridges) on the screen. You then select the appropriate ones and PEP does the rest. So now it's possible to mix and match a variety of fonts within the same Printer Action Table. (For further information on fonts and cartridges, *see* page 75.)

> The Pep has WYSIWYG preview which allows you to see what a page or document looks like before it prints. The feature makes it possible for you to check centred text and adjust margins, spacing, layout and try out different typestyles, amongst other things

The PEP has WYSIWYG (What You See Is What You Get) preview which allows you to see what a page or document looks like before it prints. The feature makes it possible for you to check centred text and adjust margins, spacing, layout and try out different typestyles, amongst other things. This will save a lot of time previously spent on guesswork.

There is something called a lightbar select feature, also known as 'point and shoot'. Here, documents can be loaded by moving the lightbar to the name of the file displayed and pressing the function key F10. The document you want is then immediately accessed. PEP can also display an entire directory tree for a specified drive by pressing one key.

Pull down menus have been expanded with many new selections, giving you the option to bypass the main menu.

CONNECTING A PRINTER TO YOUR SYSTEM 53

Keystroke combinations are now displayed on the pull down menu next to selectable functions for faster learning. The most frequently modified print options are now on a screen by themselves with the remaining options on a second screen.

The print spool feature allows you to continue working on a document while it's still printing, eliminating the wait for documents to leave the print queue.

The company Bitstream's Fontware Installation Kit, plus various screen fonts, are included free with PEP. The screen fonts are used to display documents on the screen, just as they will appear when printed.

A variety of Bitstream's proportionally spaced screen fonts in Swiss (similar to Helvetica) and Dutch (similar to Times Roman) are included in 8, 10, 12 and 14 point, in regular, bold and italic typestyles. Swiss and Dutch fonts (for screen and printer) in any size can be created with the Fontware Installation Kit provided. Additional screen and printer typefaces can be purchased directly from Fontware itself.

The above information about PEP is intended as an illustration of the previous few pages and the levels of sophistication that are currently being attained. It can all be done now. All you need to be using is MultiMate Advantage II, 384k available RAM (random access memory), a hard disk and DOS Version 3.1 or higher. It's also desirable (but not necessarily mandatory) to be using a laser printer.

To reiterate the point made at the beginning of this example, the software manufacturers are now supplying software with many printer drivers incorporated. Remember too that the computer industry is still very young, so further dramatic developments are likely.

LOOKING AFTER THE PRINTER

It might seem obvious but you'd be surprised how many people ignore basic advice and stick their printers in dusty, greasy or damp places. One person placed his printer on a window ledge in a non-air conditioned office block with windows which faced south. Admittedly not everyone would go to this extreme, nor would everyone suffer such hot-house conditions. The printer in question was left unattended for many hours (no-one actually knew for how long) which resulted in a severely distorted casing, buckled circuit boards and a sticky paper roller.

Not only should one avoid putting printers in direct sunlight, but near any source of heat. The normal 'safe' temperature range is quoted at 5°C to 25°C, although the latter figure can vary.

At the large end of the marketplace, there are companies specialising in maintaining printers, but at the lower end how should you look after your 300 dot matrix printer or your 1,200 'special offer' laser? You can either take a risk and do nothing, or you can take out a maintenance contract through the supplier of your system. There are many organisations to choose from and word of mouth can be a good provider of advice and information.

Whatever is decided, whether it be in-house maintenance, third party service agent, manufacturer supplied or nothing at all, there are a few basic steps that should be taken to keep the printer clean.

With matrix printers, daisywheels, thermal transfer and ink jet, the unit should be given a thorough clean. Unplug the power supply, remove any paper and the ribbon, where fitted. Using a soft brush and a vacuum cleaner with a small nozzle, clean the unit and try to clear away all the paper dust.

The print head can be moved safely with the power off, but if you are cleaning a matrix printer, make sure the print head has cooled before you touch it, as it gets very hot. Care should also be taken not to bend or damage any of the parts inside the unit.

If the outer casing of the printer gets very dirty, you can clean it with a soft, clean cloth dampened with a mild detergent dissolved in water. Again, switch off and unplug the unit, and ensure that water doesn't get inside the printer.

Don't use a hard brush or abrasive cloth. Never use alcohol or a thinner to clean the printer because it could damage the print head and the case. Oil should not be sprayed on the inside of the printer, as this may damage the mechanism.

It is a good idea to place a label somewhere on the printer, when you've finished cleaning the unit, to note when you last cleaned the unit and when it needs doing again.

Place a label on your printer to note when you last cleaned the unit and when it needs doing again

MAINTAINING THE MATRIX PRINT HEAD

The print head of a matrix printer will not usually require any maintenance. The only time you'll need to touch it is when changing the ribbon or cleaning the printer.

When the printer is working, the print head gets very hot. Never move the printer when it is switched on, and never touch it immediately after printing. When changing the ribbon, for example, switch the printer off first and let it cool down for a few minutes.

The pace of development in print head technology has been rapid. Indeed with an ordinary black ribbon, the print head should last for some 100 million characters, which translates into over 50,000 pages of text. If the print head should fail, you'll see the results of one or more of the pins firing erratically - your printout will be patchy. However, if you experience a patchy printout suddenly or long before the expected lifetime is up, your problems won't be to do with the head but another component in the unit.

This can also be true of thermal transfer type printers. Ink jet print heads require specialist attention, so don't try sticking paper clips or pens or whatever into the works to ungum a sticky head. Remember that with ink jet and thermal printers, the paper is not physically touched by the print head.

Daisywheels are a lot easier - to understand and handle, and clean.

Check that your printer has a manual (hopefully it'll be a clearly laid out one), and keep it close to the printer. And refer to it whenever you have any doubts.

MAINTAINING LASER PRINTERS

Modern laser printers are usually designed to be 'user friendly', allowing easy access to all parts of the equipment.

If a fault does occur during the guarantee period, you should know whether it's the manufacturer or the dealer who is responsible for the handling of claims under guarantee, and for how long it is covered. If a fault occurs outside the guarantee period, check your maintenance contract - or rather, make sure you've got a main-tenance contract. There are all sorts on offer.

Generally speaking, the working life of individual components has to be considered as well. When there's a fault which can only be repaired back in a specialist workshop, you must know who's going to be doing the work and how long it's going to take. You'll also have to check whether a replacement printer will be made available for you.

Modern laser printers are usually designed to be 'user friendly', allowing easy access to all parts of the equipment

Maintenance is covered in Chapter 7.

PROGRAMMING THE PRINTER - THE FACILITIES YOU GET

The purpose of the following section is to describe and inform; not to deter! Indeed, many users will not need to know how to program their printer, and can therefore skip straight to page 69.)

A modern printer will be delivered with 'default' settings programmed in, e.g. current paper position becomes the top of page; released left and right margin; vertical tab channel of zero; horizontal tab settings every eight characters; left justification; and last font in the font family set from the front panel. It is possible to change these default settings by programming the printer, eg copy ROM (read only memory) character set to user defined characters, set n/180 line feed pitch, select italic characters, select 8 bit double speed double density bit image printing, select proportional printing, etc.

The manual(s) provided with your printer should give you all the information you require. But for the purposes of illustration, let us indicate the way it's tackled by Epson with its LQ-850 and LQ-1050 24-pin dot matrix printers.

There are three ways in which the printer can be initialised, or returned to a fixed set of conditions: whenever it is switched on; when it receives an INIT signal at the parallel interface (pin 31 becomes LOW); or when software sends the ESC @ command. These three types have slightly different effects - most conditions are reset in all cases, but some are only reset when the printer is turned on or when it receives an INIT signal.

The conditions which are always reset at power on, or when the printer receives an INIT signal (hardware initialisation) are: the print head returns to its home position, the interface signals are reset, the printer is put on-line, the print buffer is cleared, the input buffer is cleared, the download character set is cleared and the printer's default values are restored. Initialisation with ESC @ (software initialisation) will only: clear the print buffer, restore default values, deselect download characters and reset panel settings to the last ones selected.

Commands can be given in the format ESC/P where /P represents a variable factor, and they are available in either draft or letter quality typestyle. So consider the example ESC EM, which refers to a command which must be given at the beginning of a page, and which is used to select the optional cut sheet feeder according to the value of the variable m:

Format ASCII	ESC	EM	m
decimal	27	25	m
exadecimal	1B	19	m
keyboard	CTRL [	CTRL Y	m

CONNECTING A PRINTER TO YOUR SYSTEM 59

m	dec	hex	function
0	48	30	turns the mode off
4	52	34	turns the mode on
R	82	52	ejects a sheet without loading

The command is only valid if a particular cut sheet feeder is fitted and will in any case be ignored if a value other than those specified is used.

In this example, the formats shown refer to the sequence in standard ASCII characters, decimal numbers, hexadecimal numbers and keyboard characters respectively. All four formats are equivalent and it should be easy to pick the one most suited to your purpose.

For example, a BASIC programmer might refer to the decimal format, whereas somebody using a word processor might refer to the decimal or hexadecimal format during an installation of the program. In the same way, a machine code programmer would use the hexadecimal format. Entering the sequence from the keyboard as in the keyboard format may be possible in some software. The keyboard format shows the series of keys which should be pressed to input the code directly from the keyboard of the computer - it is not suitable in all situations.

This method, it should be said, includes ASCII characters which do not represent letters or symbols and cannot be found on the keyboard. These codes can be given by holding down the control key and pressing one of the normal keys. So, CTRL [means hold down the control key and press [.

However, some applications programs have their own uses for control key sequences and these should not be confused with the control key values set for a particular command. You may not be able to use the keyboard format method of input in these cases, unless special provision is made for entering codes this way in the software.

> Some applications programs have their own uses for control key sequences and these should not be confused with the control key values set for a particular command

In the example ESC EM just quoted, the command ESC EM R ejects the current sheet of paper without loading a new one. When the cut sheet mode is selected, paper is loaded automatically by form feed commands and also by line feeds, vertical tabs or ESC J commands if the final print position lies outside the print area. Data can then be sent to the printer continuously, in the same way as when continuous paper is being used.

For example, to select the cut sheet feeder you would send the following codes:

ASCII: ESC   EM   4

decimal: 27   25   52

hexadecimal: 1B   19   34

keyboard: CTRL [CTRL Y   4

With these particular printers, ESC/P commands are grouped into various classes: printer operation commands, data control commands, line feeding, formatting commands, word-processing commands, print style commands, print size and character width commands, print enhancement commands,

CONNECTING A PRINTER TO YOUR SYSTEM 61

character set commands and graphics (bit image) commands.

Consider the character set command to select an international character set, ESC R. Some character codes can be made to produce different characters for different countries. There are 24 ASCII codes that can represent more than one character each. You determine which each is to stand for by selecting one of the available character sets.

ASCII: ESC   R   n

decimal: 27   82   n

hexadecimal: 1B   52   n

keyboard: CTRL [r   n

The value of n determines which character set is printed, as shown below.

n	country	n	country
0	USA	7	Spain I
1	France	8	Japan
2	Germany	9	Norway
3	United Kingdom	10	Denmark II
4	Denmark/Norway I	11	Spain II
5	Sweden	12	Latin America
6	Italy	64	Legal

To select the international character set for the UK for example, you would send the following sequence to the printer:

ASCII: ESC   R   ETX

decimal: 27   82   3

hexadecimal: 1B   52   03

keyboard: CTRL [W   CTRL C

There are two wordprocessing commands which are intended for word processor software writers to use in positioning the characters on the line: ESC SP and ESC a. ESC SP sets the intercharacter space while ESC a selects the justification mode.

With ESC SP the size of the space printed between characters is increased by n units and is in addition to the spaces already allowed for in the definition of the character. The value of n should be in the range 0 to 127.

ASCII: ESC   SP   n

decimal: 27   32   n

hexadecimal: 1B   20   n

The amount of space between characters varies with the character mode:

mode   *unit*

draft 10 pitch, 12 pitch or 15 pitch   1/120 inch

CONNECTING A PRINTER TO YOUR SYSTEM 63

condensed draft 10 pitch or 12 pitch   1/240 inch

LQ 10 pitch, 12 pitch, 15 pitch or proportional   1/180 inch

LQ proportional superscript/subscript   1/180 inch

condensed LQ 10 pitch, 12 pitch or proportional   1/360 inch

condensed LQ proportional superscript/subscript   1/360 inch

To set the intercharacter space to 60 units, for example, you would send the following to the printer:

ASCII: ESC   SP   ≥

decimal: 27   32   60

hexadecimal: 1B   20   3C

Justification is often performed by a word processor. The command ESC a causes text to be justified automatically by the printer. The term justification refers to headings which are centred on a line, or text printed so that the margins line up on the right, on the left or both.

ASCII: ESC   a   m

decimal: 27   97   m

hexadecimal: 1B   61   m

The type of justification set depends on the value of m, which can be sent as an ASCII code in the range 1 to 4 or as the characters 0 to 4.

m   justification mode

0   left (the default)

1   centre

2   right

3   full

Justification is then carried out between the margins whenever the printer receives a CR, LF, VT or FF code or when printed because the buffer becomes full. (CR = carriage return command, LF = line feed, VT = tab vertically and FF = form feed.)

The ESC a command should always be placed at the beginning of a new line, as all data preceding it on the same line is lost. If m has the value 3, there should be no carriage returns in a paragraph. If bit imaging printing is mixed with text, justification will not be carried out properly. Also, the HT (tab horizontally) and ESC $ (set absolute dot position) commands are ignored if m has the value 1 or 2. If received while using justified printing, data following the code is justified.

If full justification is selected then:

- negative values for relative print position are ignored

- justification is only effective for lines with a length of 75 per cent to 125 per cent of the distance between the left and right margin; otherwise lines are printed flush left

- justification is done by changing the word space (not including any increment or decrement set for print pitch). Character spacing can be increased up to twice the normal

CONNECTING A PRINTER TO YOUR SYSTEM 65

width or decreased to a 1/4 of the normal width. But if these changes are not enough to justify the line, the text is printed flush left.

When m = 1 or 2, negative values for relative print positions are ignored.

To set centre justification you would send the following codes to the printer:

ASCII: ESC   a   1

decimal: 27   97   49

hexadecimal: 1B   61   31

Some commands allow a variable input, the most common of which is to use one of two characters to switch a particular function on or off. This is normally the character 0 for off and 1 for on. The characters 0 and 1 or the characters with ASCII codes 0 and 1 can be used in these commands and the possibilities are detailed in the following table:

	turn off	*turn off*	*turn on*	*turn on*
ASCII:	NUL	0	SOH	1
decimal:	0	48	1	49
hexadecimal:	00	30	01	31
keyboard:	CTRL @	0	CTRL A	1

It should be pointed out that the summary only shows the variable n, and if n = 0 it turns off and if n = 1 it turns on. To use double printing continuously the code format is as detailed in the following table:

ASCII:	ESC	W	n
decimal:	27	87	n
hexadecimal:	1B	57	n
keyboard:	CTRL [	W	n

In this case n can be either 1 or 0, to begin or end double width printing. To turn on enlarged print from BASIC using the ASCII codes the command could be either of the following lines:

LPRINT CHR$(27); CHR$(87); CHR$(1);

LPRINT CHR$(27); 'W'; CHR$(1);

To turn it on using the actual character 1, the BASIC command could be either of the following lines:

LPRINT CHR$(27); CHR$(87); CHR$(48);

LPRINT CHR$(27); 'W1';

If the software package you are using permits commands to be input from the keyboard, the key sequence to turn double width printing on would be:

CTRL [, followed by W, followed by CTRL A, or

CTRL [, followed by W, followed by 1

CONNECTING A PRINTER TO YOUR SYSTEM 67

In ASCII terms they correspond to using the sequence ESC W SOH or ESC W 1.

Where the command uses the last item to indicate whether a feature should be turned on or off, either the ASCII codes 0 and 1, or the ASCII characters 0 and 1, can be sent. This is not always the case with more complex commands where the data can take a range of values and therefore has to be given in the form of ASCII codes.

Some sequences contain variables which can take a range of values, which is usually the range 0 to 127 inclusive. For example, to set the page length in lines the format is:

ASCII:	ESC	C	n
decimal:	27	67	n
hexadecimal:	1B	43	n
keyboard:	CTRL [	C	n

In this case n can have a value from 0 to 127 inclusive. When a software package permits input directly from the keyboard, the key to be pressed depends on the number of lines required. For example, to set the page length to 24 lines you would type CTRL [then C then CTRL X. To set the page length to 66 lines, you should type CTRL [then C then B. Particular variables associated with the keys to be pressed for your printer will be detailed in relevant sections of the manual(s).

CHAPTER 4

DESKTOP PUBLISHING AND NETWORKING

DESKTOP PUBLISHING

Desktop publishing (DTP), otherwise known as electronic publishing, corporate electronic publishing or computer-aided publishing (or whatever) has been around essentially since 1985. That's the time Aldus introduced its PageMaker software package for the Apple Macintosh microcomputer.

It actually goes back further still. DTP, or the production of printed material from your desk started in the 1970s when Xerox first marketed the Alto workstation with a laser printer. Today, of course, there are many flourishing businesses sporting a DTP set up and obligatory laser printer.

It seems as if the whole computer industry has caught DTP fever. You can buy a DTP package from just about every computer company today although the two dominant varieties appear to be PageMaker and Ventura Publisher.

If you were to walk into a computer shop and buy a DTP system, what you'd get for your money is a personal computer with graphics capability, plus (preferably) a full or two page screen display, the relevant software package and a laser printer. You would probably expect to pay about the £8,000 mark, but there are always systems available for less. Expect to pay more for extras such as a scanner for converting drawings, diagrams, logos and photos/pictures into a computer readable format.

WYSIWYG

You may come across the acronym WYSIWYG, ie What You See Is What You Get. This refers to the image you see on your computer's screen. If you have a high graphic resolution

DESKTOP PUBLISHING AND NETWORKING   71

screen, you can see exactly what the printout will look like before you print it out. This incidentally applies to the selected format (portrait or landscape display); the various fonts in different point sizes; and the graphics, drawings or photographs that are included. So, the report, magazine or whatever you are producing on your system can be viewed clearly before you print it. This is WYSIWYG.

The applications of DTP systems fall into two camps on the whole: in-house publishing (of reports, sales leaflets, documentation, catalogues, newsletters, forms, business reports and presentation documents) and commercial publishing (of magazines, books, newspapers, catalogues, lists, handbooks and instruction manuals).

WYSIWYG stands for What You See Is What You Get - it refers to the image on the computer screen. If you have a high graphic resolution screen, you can see exactly what the printout will look like before you print it out

It is interesting to compare the production processes involved in DTP and the existing conventional production process:

- with DTP, an author prepares his or her article on a personal computer with the help of a wordprocessing package. This text is subsequently corrected on the personal computer and edited to the required and correct length. Following this, page make up is handled directly on screen as well. Using a software layout program, text and graphics can be combined and placed on to the page. The laser printer produces the finished page and the photographs can then be located in their places. The pages are then ready for the printer. (Please note that DTP doesn't produce the magazine; a magazine printer does that. DTP produces camera ready artwork, which the magazine printer uses to make printing plates.)

- with the conventional process, the author again writes his or her article with the help of a wordprocessing package. The subsequent printed out text is edited, marked-up for style and sent to the typesetter. The composed text is returned from the compositor in the form of a galley proof. The layout is then created by cutting and pasting the galley proof onto a layout sheet. After the galley proof has been corrected and edited to the required length, according to the layout, everything is returned to the typesetter for correction. The corrected material together with photos and any graphic material is then pasted up as artwork. The pages are then ready for the magazine printer.

Economy and capabilities. It can be seen that by using the DTP approach, both time and money are saved, often in very appreciable quantities. And the process is simplified too. All that remains now is for direct communications links to be set up between individual DTP systems and the printer. Technology makes it possible to do this today, but costs and other matters preclude such availability to the likes of the business community. But it will come.

RESOLUTION

To obtain reproduction to what is practically typeset quality and graphical accuracy very much depends on the resolution of the printout. It should be realised that the professionals in the phototypesetting business are working with equipment that gives them a resolution anywhere from 600 to 2,500 dots per inch.

The resolution of commercially-marketed laser printers (as well as those in corporate computer centres) is 300 dots per inch. For the majority of applications - such as DTP work or mass mailing letters from a building society - this resolution allows a print quality that is more than adequate. To increase

DESKTOP PUBLISHING AND NETWORKING 73

the quality to 400 dots per inch, the laser would have to double its memory. Add to this the call for an even greater precision in components' manufacture, and the high price of 400 dots per inch machines is put into context.

PAGE DESCRIPTION LANGUAGES

Within a laser printer, the role of its page description language is to translate the content of a document into a digital character sequence. This makes up the format in the printer as a bit map display of vector graphics. Today, there are over 100 different page description languages on the market, most of which are adapted to specific systems. Once again, however, there are really only two important languages - PostScript and Prescribe - the others differing from them only in minor ways.

There are really only two important languages - Postscript and Prescribe - the other languages differing from them only in minor ways

PostScript, marketed by the Adobe Company and offered by the larger manufacturers of personal computers, such as Apple and IBM, as a standard page description language, started life in the 1970s. PostScript operates with 'user friendly' interface software such as GEM or Microsoft Windows to prepare the printed page. Behind the interface run DTP software packages such as Ventura or PageMaker, which determine precisely at which point on the page the words and graphics should be placed.

Graphics are constituted from lines, circles, grids, grey shade scaling and drawings, all generated in the computer, as well as photographs and logos, which are introduced to the system through a scanner.

74 PROFITING FROM YOUR PRINTER

As PostScript, like the BASIC language, is an interpretive language, the statements are not turned into machine language until program execution. However, this activity does not take place in the system computer, but in a special computer incorporated into the laser printer. This separation of duties goes most of the way to explaining why PostScript capable laser printers are more expensive than standard laser printers.

The PostScript page description language was incorporated by Apple into its Laserwriter in 1985 and since then the two products have become synonymous. Sales of laser printers equipped with PostScript increased by 107 per cent from 1987 with the development of PostScript clones, PostScript upgrade cards and alternative page description languages complicating matters. Whereas in 1987 the Apple Laserwriter accounted for 69 per cent of total PostScript sales this figure had increased to 70 per cent in 1988, represented by the Laserwriter IINT and Laserwriter IINTX, the successor to the Laserwriter. Sales of PostScript equipped printers accounted for 16.5 per cent of all laser units sold in 1988.

Prescribe works in a similar way to Postscript, but you can program and create the final layout of the printout by yourself. Commands within the page description language, embedded into the text of a document (and separated from it by control codes) are directly converted during the print out

Prescribe works in a similar way to PostScript, but you can program and create the final layout of the printout by yourself. Commands within the page description language, embedded into the text of a document (and separated from it by control codes) are directly converted during the printout.

For example, the Prescribe program, you can use a totally different typeface for a header on a document, from that used in the main body of the text. You can also program your own dynamic fonts, produce business forms, draw company logos, define bar codes, create vector graphics, write codes for additional printer emulations, develop interfaces with special programs and many other developments. For the creation of new fonts however, a font editor is provided.

FONTS

For text, printers rely on fonts to give them the necessary information regarding the shape and size of each character they print. It is important for you to look at the range and types of fonts that are available as these affect the appearance of your work as much as print quality itself. It is necessary for you to understand what is meant by professional terms like type font or style, type size and character set.

It is important to realise that a typestyle is a subset of a typeface. There are three type styles: Roman, sans serif and Gothic. Roman faces are among the most frequently used in wordprocessing or DTP, with every letter beginning and ending with small horizontal closing lines. Known as serifs, these lines guide your eyes within the text.

A typestyle is a subset of a typeface. There are three type styles: Roman, sans serif and Gothic. Roman faces are among the most frequently used in wordprocessing or DTP

If you were to opt for a clear and modern look to your text, you would choose a sans serif font such as Helvetica. Gothic texts are very rarely used today and can only be found in the title of daily papers or perhaps to decorate the beginning of a chapter in a heavy tome.

Next to be tackled is the type family. The Roman grouping includes the Times, Garamond, Bookman, Palatino and Bodoni, while sans serif types include Helvetica, Futura, Avant Garde and jobbing script.

Within a single typeface there are different styles such as light, thin, medium, bold, extra bold, plus the same in italics.

When you are looking at font numbers, the trap to avoid is looking for different type**faces** rather than different type**styles** when you're looking at font numbers. The manufacturers will wax lyrical about the wondrous number of fonts their machines possess. All printers have some resident fonts but many will enable you to add extra ones through inserting font cartridges or cards. These will occasionally contain extra random access memory or emulations, and are plugged into the printer when it is switched off.

All printers have some resident fonts but many will enable you to add extra ones through inserting font cartridges or cards

If this approach is not offered or if it's not available, the alternative is to download the font from the computer's memory (having put it there first via a floppy disk) to the printer's memory. Depending on the memory your printer possesses, you can add many more fonts at any one time, plus the fonts are normally cheaper and the library of available fonts very much greater than with cartridges or cards. The disadvantage is that the font is lost when the printer is switched off. So you have to add it again when you switch on. These are called **soft fonts**.

An example then is that 10 pitch Times is different from 10 pitch Times Bold or Italic, or from 12 pitch Times. So look for a typeface and don't be swayed by a typestyle. A better visual result is often attained by using various typestyles within one typeface, rather than mixing many different typefaces.

TYPE SIZES

Type sizes are measured in points, with 72 points to the inch. The height of a face is determined from the height of initial letters and the height of capitals. The distance between individual characters is either defined as a fixed division - for example, 10 characters per inch - independent of the actual width of any particular character, or a proportional division or spacing where the letters and numbers are arranged according to their relative dimensions.

For example, an 'l' will take up less space than an 'm', a 't' will take up less space than a 'w'. So a word such as 'accommodate' takes up more space than another 11 letter word not possessing the double 'm'.

The layout of the resulting sheet of paper is determined by the alignment of the text horizontally or vertically. This is known as portrait or landscape format.

A font may be defined as a specific type family with a specific typeface in a given point size. Examples of this are: Helvetica Medium 10 Point, Times Light Italic 12 Point, Avant Garde Extra Bold 12 Point, etc. The term 'character set', which you will undoubtedly come across, refers only to the number and meaning of the available characters (that is the letters, figures, punctuation marks and symbols). It does not refer to their graphic presentation in any way.

Many factors contribute to the process which determines the typefaces chosen. Creativity is a wonderful gift that cannot be won or earned. Use of medium, bold or italic and variations of

78 PROFITING FROM YOUR PRINTER

these can go some way to compensate for any lack of real design ability. In the hands of a good creator, many fine works can be produced.

Print sizes can be small, medium or large; schemes can be plain or ordinary, x-bolded or y-bolded; slopes of characters can be negative (ie to the left), zero (ie upright or ordinary) or positive (ie to the right); characters can be compressed together, normal or expanded; and characters can be rotated by 90, 180 or 270 degrees.

These are all possible through the use of **dynamic** fonts - these are in addition to the standard typefaces which are obtained by using the **resident fonts**, and are loaded dynamically into the permanent memory. With a resident font you can only use the typeface as it is supplied, but with a dynamic font you can do all the things mentioned above. Totally new faces or styles can be created by amending the dynamic fonts so that they assume new shapes and sizes.

Individual typefaces can be changed further by using certain additional parameters. The company Kyocera for example offers three dynamic fonts which are arranged as proportional scripts and are recommended for creating very large characters or special effects. Thus, it is possible that headings can be printed with large letters and paragraphs opened with oversized 'drop capitals'. In addition, special creative effects can be achieved by the processes of zooming and stretching.

It is easy to develop and create such designs as company symbols and logos on a computer system. The rough is transformed into graphics on a screen - and any inaccuracies that are seen can be reworked pixel by pixel

It is easy to develop and create such designs as company symbols and logos on a computer system. The first stage or rough is transformed into graphics on a screen. Here, the graphics has to be initially generated by special commands as a point pattern. If there is an original already to hand, graphic characters can be read into the system via an electronics gadget called a scanner. Any inaccuracies that are seen can be reworked pixel (picture point size) by pixel.

Your own scripts and special characters can also be created in this way, for which it is mandatory that a page description language is used. Finished designs of logos, signatures, symbols or forms can then be stored on IC cards and can be loaded straight into the laser printer.

The scanner system mentioned above can bring into your system all special logos, drawings, photographs, etc, to complement existing text and graphics. Your original (logo or whatever) is scanned by photoelectric diodes or charge coupled device (CCD) elements point by point with a resolution of up to 800-by-800 dots per inch. The detected light/dark information is digitally coded in up to 32 shades of grey, transferred to the memory of the system computer and stored there as a digital 'image'. As a result, pictures within a text or layout can be processed further and printed out as part of another document through a laser printer.

Lasers have the ability to make much more use of different typestyles. Indeed this is one of their major advantages, although the capabilities of the latest inkjet and thermal transfer printers now equal many if not all of their font capabilities

So, for text, printers depend on fonts to provide them with the necessary data regarding the shape and size of each character they print. It is then up to you to assess the range and types of fonts on offer as they will directly affect your finished products, as much as the print quality you'll end up with. Remember, lasers have the ability to make much more use of different typestyles. Indeed this is one of their major advantages, although the capabilities of the latest inkjet and thermal transfer printers now equal many if not all of their font capabilities.

PRINTING - THE ACHILLES HEEL OF NETWORKING

Printers are getting - indeed have got - much faster, and with this increased speed and sophistication has come the requirement for a printer to serve several computers or workstations. To be practical, the efficient way to achieve this is to bolt the printer into a local area network. However, this only works if the primary reason you are setting up the local area network is for data purposes and exchanging data, and not for sharing printers. It's much too expensive (and ridiculous) for that.

Printing has long been viewed as the Achilles Heel of networking

Printing has long been viewed as the Achilles Heel of networking. Within a specialist finance house in the City for example, the day's trading is proceeding efficiently and brokers are working busily at their high powered workstations plotting currency flows, watching spot markets, buying, selling and whatever else keeps them busy. Suddenly, three of them want printouts, each say four pages long. Then a manager needs a draft of his monthly report. A secretary has to send out three letters, each two pages long with the first on headed notepaper. The envelopes will be done on an electric typewriter (yes, they still have their uses).

DESKTOP PUBLISHING AND NETWORKING 81

Suddenly everyone wants their printout from the printer

A jam will occur. Not with the printer, although if that develops a fault there would be real havoc. The group will gather around the laser printer, wondering who is going to be the first to receive their copy.

Someone will have fed in the wrong paper. The wrong font size might have been specified from the previous print run. The whole set up of the printer may be wrong.

You may even have chosen to do a print out of three sheets on company headed notepaper only to find that someone from the support group is doing a mass mailing exercise of 100 plain sheets. Or, that person has just finished and forgotten to replace the 'right' paper in the proper bins.

Only now are people beginning to focus attention on this problem area. However, it is possible to run 'normal' services. Currently, in any situations which might become difficult, there are routines and procedures set up to overcome any difficulties. Talk to your printer supplier for the latest information on developments, because there is intense activity within the printer manufacturers' research departments.

CHAPTER 5

PAPER HANDLING

There are several different types and sizes of paper that can be used with printers generally. It all boils down to the sort of printer you've got connected to your system. As well as printing on single (or 'cut') sheets and continuous (or 'fanfold') paper, it's possible to print on envelopes, labels, plastic film and even sandpaper.

In this chapter we'll be examining the different ways of controlling paper flow through different types of printer system: paper slew rates; tractor mechanisms and sprocket feeding systems; adjusting paper tension; what to look out for when deciding what type of paper to choose; what all the terminology means; printing on different media; sheet-feeding devices; plus all the mechanical bits that people hadn't thought of before (and in many cases, probably didn't know existed).

If anyone thought all you had to do was buy a printer and stick some reasonably attractive looking paper through it, and wait for the crisp and clean copy to come bursting through, they're in for a shock. The following gives useful advice for dealing with practical problems that can occur with printers.

TO CUT OR FANFOLD

The major difference between all the printer technologies really comes down to the type of stationery system employed - single, cut sheets or continuous, fanfold paper or a user-defined choice of either through the same printer.

The major difference between all the printer technologies really comes down to the type of stationery system employed

If you opt for laser printer technology at the 8 to 12 pages per minute level (and that includes light emitting diode and liquid crystal shutter technologies too), then you're stuck with single sheets. Usually, that means A4 size, although A3 capability units are coming on to the market. The lion's share will still be in the A4 camp though. Some units also offer the facility of double sided printing which has obvious economy spin-offs, and a good neatness factor which is useful when preparing reports.

All laser printers come equipped with reasonably easy-to-handle paper trays, which are similar to, but a bit better than photocopier type trays.

The disadvantage of the lasers - for all the glory they seem to attract - is that they cannot (currently) handle continuous stationery, although if you're talking about a laser working at 90 to 100 pages per minute, it's a different story. Another disadvantage is that you cannot use multi-part stationery. If, however, all you're using your laser for is to print invoices, then you could have saved yourself money by buying a less sophisticated machine. To produce invoices, only a relatively cheap matrix printer is required - and a 9-pin one at that.

> The disadvantage of the lasers - for all the glory they seem to attract - is that they cannot handle continuous stationery, although if you're talking about a laser working at 90 to 100 pages per minute, it's a different story. Another disadvantage is that you cannot use multi-part stationery

Looking at other technologies, like dot matrix, thermal transfer, daisywheel, inkjet (of whatever category - solid ink pellets or reservoir), shuttle matrix, band, ion deposition, magnetographic and high speed laser, the first four can (usually but not exclusively) take either cut sheet or fanfold. The latter five, if only by dint of their speeds of throughput, will generally only lend themselves to continuous throughput.

Matrix, daisy, ink and thermal types of printer will all be equipped with a platen, similar to that used in the typewriter. All you have to do is feed in your single sheets, one at a time. This is fine if you've only got a few sheets to handle. But if, say, you have 30 sheets to pass through the printer, you've either got to have an awful lot of patience, tons of spare time and a strong arm, or you must fit what's known as a cut sheet feeder (*see also* Chapter Six on Accessories - The Hidden Costs).

This is going to cost you anything from about £150 up to £650 over the cost of what you paid for the printer. The low end of the price range covers single bin sheet feeders while the higher end reflects costs for dual bin feeders. And note that not all printers will give the option of fitting these devices.

For the uninitiated, a dual bin feeder will enable you to put company letter headed paper in one bin and clear paper in the other. Some printers will also offer the option of an envelope tray - for which a cost of about £215 may be expected. If you're using your matrix, daisywheel, inkjet or thermal transfer printer for letters and official documents, you are more likely than not going to be using cut sheets. So you really do have to look at the costs of ownership, costs per copy and the duty cycles.

Sheet feeders of whatever complexity and sophistication will cost you extra. If you are a determined non-laser (or LED or LCS) person, you must realise this point. There is also the other problem that you will not have experienced - you will need software to operate these optional sheet feeders. Then again there are stories circulating over reliability factors, so do try and see one in operation first, preferably by getting a demonstration arranged so you can check it all out.

Some inkjet devices now on the market offer single 100 sheet paper trays as standard, and some have a pin feed option too.

PAPER HANDLING 87

This is fine for letter quality stuff, but they lose out to dual bin options and envelope tray units - both in the laser and non-laser camps. It will depend on your particular application.

So the 8 to 12 pages per minute laser printer is high on the list if what you want is lots of cut sheet work, produced in letter quality and, in some cases, output with the envelopes. All have paper trays as standard and a lot, but not all, have second tray options. It will all depend on workload, your budget and awareness of what can and cannot be done.

If you're operating a 100 pages per minute laser printer or a 900 lines per minute band printer, you will obviously be using continuous stationery which will be shooting through the system at an alarming rate. It's all very well having the paper feeding in at one end, but just think what you've got to do with it at the other. A whole new world opens up - it's the domain of power stackers and efficient paper handling.

If you are working in a local area network environment, with a medium-sized computer system or in a large mainframe installation, a lot of this may be a bit basic for you.

Taking the local area network camp, a referral back to Chapter Four is in order. Printing is without doubt the Achilles Heel of networking. The network manager will probably be aware of the complexities of providing printing stations that are to be used for headed letter paper, and ones that are to be used for internal reports and everyday company work. The individuals at their workstations are probably not so aware of the problems.

> Printing is without doubt the Achilles Heel of Networking. The network manager will probably be aware of the complexities of providing printing stations that are to be used for headed letter paper, and ones that are to be used for internal reports and everyday company work

In the medium-range market, the computer manager will probably be aware of the types of printer that he or she can and cannot connect, and what he or she needs to provide so that management can get what they want out of his department. A similar story will apply to the data processing manager, or management information systems manager, of the large mainframe installation.

MOVING AND HANDLING CONTINUOUS STATIONERY

With many of the non-laser (ie 8 to 12 pages per minute) printers and some ink jets, plus the options on some daisywheel devices, special equipment is needed to handle the continuous stationery. Known as tractor feeders, these can be split up into the following groups: pin feed mechanisms, tractor feed mechanisms, push feed tractors, and pull feed tractors.

Pin feed mechanisms - basically a ring of sprockets which run around both sides of the platen. They are usually adjustable to compensate for different widths of paper, but they are not too good at handling such paper as labels and multi-part forms. The problem is that there are not enough sprockets to grasp all the holes in the paper at any particular time.

Tractor feed mechanisms are a refinement of the above. A number of sprockets are arranged on a revolving belt and the sprockets grab the holes in the stationery to enable several holes to be engaged simultaneously. This compares favourably with the one or two holes engaged by the pin feed mechanism and makes for less paper slippage and a stronger registration.

PAPER HANDLING 89

Push feed tractors are very easy to operate. The paper is pushed through from behind the platen and because of this the system permits a short tear-off of paper at a perforation. A disadvantage of this system can be that it may be less suited to handling heavy stationery (like labels) as they cannot be used with bottom fed paper, which has to be pulled up through the printer.

Pull feed tractors grab the paper once it's gone round the platen. These are then harder to load with paper and don't allow you to take the last printed page out of the printer without making an extra form feed, which can be wasteful if you're doing several small print runs. In some systems you'll end up having to take all the paper out of the printer. Looking on the positive side, these systems can work with a bottom or front feed slot. This is an arrangement which permits a straighter paper path.

> There is a slot at the base or the front of each printer through which the continuous stationery is passed. In most cases, paper comes in through the rear and is then passed around the platen. To feed paper from below results in a straighter paper path, which means fewer paper jams

Poring over your printer's instruction manual, you may come across the term 'push/pull tractor'. This is not a reference to a tractor feed mechanism which can be adjusted for use as a push feed or pull feed tractor.

There is a slot at the base or the front of each printer through which the continuous stationery is passed. In most cases, paper comes in through the rear and is then passed around the platen. To feed paper from below results in a straighter paper path, which means fewer paper jams. Some users may be equipped with printers that offer that useful feature of **paper parking**, which is a boon to those users who don't like to change the paper more often than is absolutely necessary.

This facility is not offered on all printers. Basically, what happens is that the fanfold paper is reversed until it clears the platen. A single cut sheet can then be fed into the printer. Once this has been processed the fanfold paper can be put back into position. The whole process is normally controlled from the printer's control panel.

LABELS, ENVELOPES, PLASTIC AND SANDPAPER

Everyone has seen continuous rolls or sheets of labels. You can also get single sheets of labels, which are intended for use with lasers. However some users are known to have experienced all sorts of trouble with labels peeling off inside the laser mechanism and gumming up the works. Labels even get jammed up in other types of printer, even though a tractor mechanism seems to be controlling matters effectively. The advice is to ask around and seek out good quality products.

Alternatively, why not consider printing your customer's address in a relevant position on your letters and use window envelopes. But of course some people find this to be too down market or reminiscent of a bill or a demand for payment. Nevertheless it is an option worth considering.

All printers should theoretically be able to handle envelopes. However, no one technology stands supreme above the others. The thickness of envelopes can cause them to gum up the works around the platen or the internal paths of lasers. Indeed, you should be aware that the heat involved in lasers in fusing the toner on to the paper has been known to seal up envelopes. Be warned.

If you want to print on to plastic, film or, dare it be said, sandpaper, you must turn your attention to the solid inkjet printers. Apart from the quality of output, which is claimed by most to be nearly indistinguishable from that of lasers, they are the only devices that could cope with such esoteric applications.

Ink jet technology uses only as much ink as is necessary to make an image and possesses the flexibility to handle both text and graphics. In fact it is also potentially the best way to put colour on to paper.

Print quality with liquid ink depends on the substrate, with the ink relying on evaporation or absorption into the paper to dry. With inkjet printers, the poorest paper gives the best print quality, whilst high rag content quality bond produces the worst.

Print quality depends on the ink's evaporation or absorption into the paper - with the inkjet printers, the poorest paper gives the best print quality

The technology's unreliability delayed large scale acceptance until the recent appearance of products from Hewlett-Packard, Canon, Dataproducts and Epson. Many of the unreliability factors are associated with clogging jets - there is the inescapable conflicting requirements of 'it must dry quickly on the paper' whilst 'it must not dry out in the printhead'. Solid ink technology is a new approach to inkjet printing: it solves the problem of liquid ink and makes it possible to develop computer printers that are versatile, reliable, cost-effective and quiet in operation.

Solid ink is a wax-based phase change material, which does not rely on the drying out of solvents to fix the image. It is fired at the paper at a higher temperature and then hardens on contact with the paper. Some ink locks into the structure of the paper while the rest stays above the paper surface, forming smooth, well-defined characters. As the ink solidifies before it can soak very far into the paper, characters remain crisp and sharp.

The key property associated with solid ink is that at room temperature it is a solid and is handled by the user as a solid. Its high optical density yields good, strong blacks and the ink has a long shelf life, with little deterioration of print quality with time.

The interaction of the ink with the paper is a key to the technology's ability to print on to a wide range of paper substrates. Furthermore, there is the ability to bond with other materials such as overhead transparency films, plastics, cardboard, tissue paper, newspaper or even sandpaper. This makes it suitable for many marking applications.

Solid ink technology is faster and quieter than daisywheel or dot matrix printing. It can print text and graphics on virtually any paper. The print quality is vastly superior to that of a dot matrix printer and it provides more paper-handling options and better print quality than laser

In practical terms, solid ink technology is faster and quieter than daisywheel or dot matrix printing. It can print text and graphics on virtually any paper. The print quality is vastly superior to that of a dot matrix printer and it provides more paper-handling options and better print quality than laser.

Producing images on to 100 per cent rag bond paper is hard to do consistently, particularly as the paper may vary in thickness as in the case of textured stock. This poses particular problems for laser printing. The difficulty lies in the transfer of an image from a uniform surface (the drum) to a non-uniform surface (the paper).

Solid ink jet technology overcomes this problem. Depending on the intended use, the formulation of the ink can be varied. For offices, the ink will need the characteristics of blackness and adhesion to substrate for the common types of paper that are used. For other applications (eg industrial marking) inks can be formulated with different characteristics. These are currently under development.

The bottom line for any printing technology is the quality of the image it produces. In terms of print quality, dot size and rate are critical factors. Consistent dot size and good dot placement provide control over the formation of the character.

The characteristics of the technology itself affect the features designed into a product. A manufacturer will create a product configuration around the basic attributes of the chosen technology.

A page-oriented technology (such as laser printing) has difficulty handling continuous forms. Solid ink technology's ability to print on such a wide range of substrates means extensive paper-handling features can be designed into the printer.

THROUGHPUT

Another technology related product attribute is throughput. Lasers must make up a complete page prior to printing. Following composition of a page, a laser printer must move the paper at a continuous speed from the start of the page to the end. In the case of a serial printer, page composition is not required prior to printing.

The look and feel of the page is a more subjective aspect of print quality. Laser technology produces output that resembles a photocopy, while with solid ink technology every page is an original.

Today's office environment demands low sound levels so that people can communicate more easily and work with less distraction. Solid ink technology offers a significant reduction in sound levels compared with dot matrix or impact character printing.

WHAT TO ASK ABOUT PAPER REQUIREMENTS

When discussing your printer requirements you will need to ask the following information to help you evaluate the products offered to you:

paper feed methods - bearing in mind what has been written before, you may want to know whether there is a built-in push feed tractor unit or whether there are two input paper trays and envelope tray; and what are the options and costs?

paper feed speed - what is it and is there adequate explanatory material in the documentation?

paper thickness - you will need to know what you can and cannot put through the device. It will vary for single sheets and continuous stationery, and also for envelopes number of copies - check maximum thickness

number of copies plus the original that can be printed, and is it continuous multi-part no carbon paper only?

paper width- will depend on you and your throughput.

PAPER HANDLING 95

As a rough guide, for 80 column type printers, it's about 7 to over 10 inches (180 to 260 mm) for cut sheets and 4 to 10 inches (101 to 254 mm) for continuous; for 132 column printers, it's 7 to over 14 inches (180 to 365 mm) for cut sheets and 4 to 16 inches (101 to 406 mm) for continuous stationery.

CHOOSING YOUR PAPER

As has already been indicated, it may not just be paper you're going to print on - but if it's a sheet of plastic film for an overhead transparency, check you've got the sort of printer that will do the job.

Once you know the width and length (for cut sheet work) of the paper to be passed through your device, certain other considerations have to be taken into account. For example, you must find out what weight of paper you can use. It's no use thinking you can stuff the company's ultra glossy and visually impressive crested and embossed letter notepaper in the machine if its weight is 120 gsm and the printer can only chug along with a maximum of 80 gsm.

> Once you know the width and length (for cut sheet work) of the paper to be passed through your device, certain other considerations have to be taken into account. For example, you must find out what weight of paper you can use

Watch out for multi-part forms too. If the printer manual tells you to use up to 82 gsm for continuous paper, it will also say to use up to 58 gsm per sheet for four copies, for example. The rule as ever is to read your manual.

Similarly, the thickness is very important too. If the company notepaper is 0.05 mm thick, you're in for a rough ride if the printer can only work with thicknesses up to 0.03 mm.

ENVELOPES

With envelopes, size is a consideration - it's no good having the wrong number envelope, eg if your printer takes Number 6 (166 mm x 92 mm) or Number 10 (240 mm x 104 mm) envelopes then that's what you need to put through it. If you really have to have different sizes, you're a candidate for labels. The quality of envelopes together with their thickness and weight have to be taken into account. Do you want bond paper, plain paper, air mail or something else? Is the thickness acceptable only up to 0.05mm (0.0197 inches) and is the weight restricted to below 90 gsm? Again, the printer's manual must be treated as a fundamental part of your system.

With labels and any other media, you should check to see whether there are any horror stories of labels gumming up the type of machine you are contemplating.

CHAPTER 6

ACCESSORIES AND CONSUMABLES - THE HIDDEN COSTS

There are many hidden costs of printer ownership. The paper, for example, that you will consume at varying rates and in varying quantities, has to be stored somewhere. Nowadays, though, you can avail yourself of the services so ably presented by various organisations who promise to deliver your 5,000 sheets of fanfold next day. They do, too.

Print ribbons run out, or rather run dry, so keeping spares is going to prove very helpful. The same applies to tapes, colour ribbons, solid ink supplies, etc.

There are costs involved in running laser printers, which you may not have thought of.

Then, there's printer stands, paper trays, envelope hoppers, paper feed attachments, acoustic hoods and sorters (anyone who has had the unenviable task of hand-collating longer documents will appreciate all this - the complete printout of a multi-page document in multiple sets can be sorted without fuss by an automatic collator).

Other items which could be considered include security (both of physical access and through software) and the cable(s) to link up with a computer.

One of the most important factors in choosing your printer is determining the choice of add-on devices available and whether they can be added to the equipment later. For example, having the right accessories can make a great difference to the performance of your laser printer.

LASER PRINTER ACCESSORIES

Once you've created your company logo, letterhead, business forms or whatever additional font, it is advisable to store them

ACCESSORIES AND CONSUMABLES - THE HIDDEN COSTS

securely using the printer command language. Almost definitely, you'll want to be able to use them again. They can be stuffed comfortably on to devices called IC cards and recalled whenever needed - and on any compatible laser printer.

The IC card (which is like the cheque card) holds a number of microchips. When the printer is switched on or when it gets a control command from the computer, the contents of one or two cards are read into the printer's integral system memory.

If you're only using your laser printer to produce text, wordprocessing and general reports, then you are only going to need a device with 512k bytes of main memory. This memory - random access memory (RAM) - will need to be expanded if pixel graphics are to be produced (as with desktop publishing, computer aided design/computer aided manufacturing, etc).

If you are creating one page (A4) of pixel graphics, your printer is going to need about 1.2 megabytes of RAM, making it wise to buy a unit that is capable of being expanded by at least 1 megabyte. A situation which all comes down to sizing again, and having a realistic future plan.

A second input paper tray is mandatory, particularly for networking applications. If you have ever had to be in a position of constantly changing the paper from first sheet letterhead to second sheet plain paper and then back again, you will appreciate a second hopper. The operating process is easily programmed to work the system.

If you have ever had to be in a position of constantly changing the paper from first sheet letterhead to second sheet plain paper and then back again, you will appreciate the importance of a second input paper tray

The main consumables for lasers are drums and toner, with subsidiary ones being developers and fuser. Many manufacturers supply the drum, toner and developer in one disposable cartridge. So when one of the consumables runs out, you replace the whole cartridge. The print drum in modern laser printers is fabricated from non-toxic substances that are safe (so don't worry when disposing of the spent cartridge).

Drum units are usually recommended to be changed at somewhere between 4,000 and 20,000 printed pages. They cost between £50 and £250. How long the unit lasts will depend on the quantity and density of print on the page. It's fair to assume that each page will contain no more than five per cent of toner for all text pages, but a lot more for graphics work. It pays to check this point out.

Toners are blessed with a uniqueness in that no-one except the printer manufacturers know their precise formulae. You get the best print the finer and smaller the individual particles are in the toner (they're composed from carbon black, resin and iron dust). In most cases, toner supply is sufficient for anything from 1,500 to 10,000 printed pages.

When printing documents with large expanses of black, it's obvious that more frequent replenishment of toner is inevitable. Indeed with some units, the drum assembly has to be changed simultaneously. Such running costs have to be taken into account when reviewing what machine you need.

The paper you are going to feed through your laser printer will have to be uncoated and dust free, which will avoid deposits occurring on the individual component parts of the unit. Rough surfaces prevent complete adhesion of toner particles, while a too smooth surface can cause the paper to slip through the take-up rollers, twist and gum up the works.

Recommended weights of the paper lie in the region of 60 to 90 gsm although you can feed heavier stuff manually. Other paper such as coloured sheets and transparencies, and labels can be used (but *see* Chapter 5). Being based on photocopier technology, any paper that is normally fed through a photocopier can be passed through a laser.

Lasers are usually given a 'life' expectancy of anywhere between 300,000 and 500,000 pages and this must be taken into account when you are looking at running costs. The chances are that you will have to replace the device after a few years and in this case a service contract with one of the many specialist companies is advisable. A laser printer is not known for its strength, although they do enjoy a better reputation than the photocopier.

> Lasers are usually given a 'life' expectancy of anywhere between 300,000 and 500,000 pages and this must be taken into account when you are looking at running costs as the chances are that you will have to replace the device

THERMAL TRANSFER PRINTER ACCESSORIES

These machines, while undoubtedly producing good quality output, are currently the most expensive printers to run. You are going to have to allow something like 10p per page just for the consumables, and it's worth bearing in mind that this does not include those other hidden costs of servicing and depreciation. Nevertheless you may feel that the quality they produce is worth the extra cost.

The print ribbons you'll need in order to operate a thermal transfer unit are very expensive. If you consider IBM's (highly acclaimed) QuietWriter, the ribbons will cost you £14.29 for

250,000 characters - so if you're cramming something in the order of 1,500 characters on your page, it will cost you 8.6p per page just for the ribbons. Add to this the fact that the thermal transfer printhead wears out very quickly, and you will have to find an extra £28 for three million characters, or 1.4p per page.

Colour printing, while an expensive and rarely-used option is nevertheless now available. Thermal transfer colour print ribbons will be expensive and so will those hidden costs of servicing and depreciation, particularly if you're the proud operator of the QMS ColorScript 100 (you won't get much change out of £20,000). The device is driven by the Mitsubishi G650 thermal transfer colour engine and is a full colour PostScript printer which can handle paper sizes up to A3.

> Thermal transfer printers have accessories such as tractor feed, single and dual bin cut cut sheet feeders and envelope trays

Thermal transfer printers have accessories such as tractor feed (eg, pull feed options), single and dual bin cut sheet feeders and envelope trays.

INK JET PRINTER ACCESSORIES

The main consumable here is, not surprisingly, ink. Also, with some devices, although print quality on different types of paper is much improved over the previous generation of ink jets, you'll still have to watch out - and be prepared to experiment.

If you're using photocopier paper with some of these units, for instance, and have taken it from the office laser printer or copier and loaded it upside down, the ink will bleed all over the place. You may not have realised that there were right and wrong sides to copier paper. But you'll find out if you use some of these printers. Of course, if you pass expensive rag bond paper through the same device, the problem will not occur.

Canon's printer, for example, uses an ink cartridge that's separate from the print head and attached by a tube, unlike Hewlett-Packard's DeskJet which has its ink cartridge on the printhead. Canon's ink cartridge life is two million characters in draft mode and replacements cost £12.

Dataproducts solid ink cartridge approach is a successful innovation with the cartridges packaged in plastic containers with a rated 420,000 character print life and a cost of £58 for 12. Diconix printers come with cartridges costing £12 for plain paper and £10 for coated ink jet paper and have claimed lives of 500,000 characters, or about 500 pages. The Hewlett-Packard DeskJet, however, uses ink that comes in a small, disposable ink cartridge/printhead combination. Costs work out at £12.83 after 350 pages of letter quality work on a 1,500 character page, or 3.7p a page.

Unfortunately, ink jet printers have suffered from a messy image in the past but the latest developments have overcome all the previous problems.

Low cost colour printing using ink jet technology is showing great promise. An existing generation of these devices is now on its way out, and will be soon replaced with innovative devices offering lower consumables costs than xerographic or thermal transfer colour printers. The most promising will probably emanate from Canon, Epson and Hewlett-Packard.

Accessories available for ink jet printers include such items as pin tractor feed options, and cut sheet feeders. But note, these are not always offered by the supplier - a point to check.

MATRIX PRINTER ACCESSORIES

Ink again plays a major part in this category, although this time it's on a ribbon. All sorts of ribbons are available; it's like a sub-culture or cottage industry. The best ribbons to go for are the multi-strike and carbon film types. If all you're doing is producing reams of drafts and low grade work, the fabric ribbons will be the best (and cheapest) option.

The main factor to look out for is the character yield you can expect to achieve. Ask around for the best source. Just because you can buy a ribbon from Jack down the road for less than you'd have to pay the local dealer, it doesn't necessarily mean you've got a good deal, as the ribbon may be of inferior quality.

Some ribbons last longer than others. Check that you've got the right one for the model of printer you've got. Some ribbons are not stocked generally, so check that the printer you're going to buy is going to allow you to shop around. Some 24-pin devices thunder along in letter quality mode and you'll be surprised how quickly the ribbon gets used up, particularly if you never use draft mode.

Matrix printers are the cheapest printer to own with low consumables costs and excellent product lives - and any matrix printer you care to name will outlive a laser

Despite this, matrix printers are the cheapest printer to own (with maybe one or two exceptions) with low consumables costs and excellent product lives. One thing's for certain - any matrix printer you care to name will outlive a laser. If you're unlucky enough to wear out a matrix printhead, however, it will unfortunately cost you a lot to have it replaced.

On the colour front, matrix printers offer the quickest, easiest and cheapest approach to colour printing. All you need to do

- after buying a matrix printer that will do it of course - is to add a colour ribbon. The only drawback is that the results are nowhere near as good as they are with thermal transfer or as they're going to be with ink jet printers.

Accessories will be such items as cut sheet feeders (some printers offer multiple bin feeders) and various tractor feed options. Then there are paper trays for output, input and binding. Acoustic hoods are marketed, although the latest printers tend to operate below irritating noise levels. There will always be a need for hoods, however, if only for security reasons. Locking the printer in an acoustically sealed environment is an obviously secure option.

DAISYWHEEL PRINTER ACCESSORIES

As with matrix printers, the daisywheel printer is one of the cheapest devices to own. However, as well as sharing the main consumable of the print ribbons (which are more expensive by dint of the fact that they're designed for high quality working), daisywheels use up their printwheels quite fast. Ribbons are usually multistrike or carbon. Accessories are such items as single and dual bin cut sheet feeders and tractor feed options.

BAND AND OTHER PRINTER ACCESSORIES

This area is the domain of the professionals, who inhabit data processing or management information services' departments, and whose workings proceed on 24 hour shifts all year long. Paper management, handling and storage is a science all of its own. At the top end of the market, teams of people are assigned to maintain large banks of printers while a company employing, say, 350 people will have a couple of staff assigned to look after the computer installation.

Many of these people will know all there is to know about changing bands on the band printer, or servicing the shuttle matrix printer, or handling the power stacker for the print run of bank statements. However, this book is intended to embrace their work, particularly as the rapid developments in the information technology markets have brought computing to ever increasing audiences. And this awareness is extending to the peripherals camp too, notably printers.

A QUIETER AND MORE ERGONOMIC FUTURE

Overall, performance is becoming increasingly better in the matrix printer business - particularly 24 and 48 pin matrix devices where the head strikes the paper, and ink jet and thermal transfer units where the heads do not strike the paper.

Many advances have been made in printer ergonomics. Covers are easy to lift up. Custom-built stands are appearing. Control panels and switches are legible, comprehensible and usable.

CHAPTER 7

PRINTER MAINTENANCE AND SERVICING

However good your printer is at churning out your workload, one day something is going to go wrong, get jammed, become worn out or simply expire. The subjects of maintenance and servicing then suddenly come very much to the fore.

Woeful cries of 'If only I'd taken out that maintenance contract, instead of skimping' or 'I never thought that would happen to me' don't mean anything when the Managing Director wants the sales forecasts 'ten minutes ago' or you need the printout for an urgent piece of work.

MANUFACTURERS' WARRANTIES

The current 'norm' vis-a-vis maintenance on computer printers is that manufacturers will grant a year's warranty and free parts and labour should there be any faults developing, with 'return to vendor' being the accepted standard. Indeed, this is the industry standard.

However, several companies are now offering **on-site** versions of this scenario free of extra charge. Some more companies are offering it as an enhancement for which you have to pay. Most of these situations are targetted at the ever-growing population of personal computer installations. In these cases, where there is a printer associated (and most will have), it too comes on to the maintenance contract.

Service contracts are offered by the dealer on behalf of his or her own repair operation. He or she may, for example, be acting as an agent for a third party company. Indeed the majority of printer maintenance work carried out on site is effected by third party companies.

In the banking environment, where investment in computer hardware is massive, particularly in central processors, disk storage and personal computer networks, the maintenance of

PRINTER MAINTENANCE AND SERVICING

the essential large laser printers is thrown in as part of the overall maintenance contract. This typifies the thinking behind many installations - the printer is just an afterthought, and not thought of in the proper context.

The printer is still that piece of equipment which produces the hard copy, the visible evidence of all your hard work. Too many people forget this fact.

Take the person in a large office environment. The printer breaks down. The personal computer is still working, the information is still held on disk. So the person thinks, 'I can get it printed out on someone else's printer!' But that person has forgotten to check the issue of compatibility, and unless he or she is prepared to spend time converting the files to ASCII files, there could be a problem. Even if the disk is converted, it may not be compatible with other disks being used in the same office . Then there's the businessperson working from home. If printing invoices, the workload has an immediacy, but if working on spreadsheets, he or she could possibly wait a couple of days if the unit broke down.

This begs the question then of whether maintenance cover needs to be instantaneous. For some people in key areas the answer is obvious, for others there may be deliberations. A service contract should always be considered. A year's on-site warranty effectively provides a free contract for the first 12 months. Warranties which only cover labour and parts may not be worth much, as sending (or taking) the printer back for service means that it is taken out of action for some time. Could you be without your printer for a minimum of five days?

Service is all about availability. It is no good having or operating hardware which is equipped with bells and whistles if it is not available for you to use. What is involved is the selling of features to enable you, the customer, to produce what you want not what the salesman or company tell you that you want

Service is all about availability. It is no good having or operating hardware which is equipped with bells and whistles if it is not available for you to use. You should be wary of what the saleperson tells you that you want, and instead look closely at what featues the machine has which will help **you** to produce what **you** want. Availability has to be guaranteed. For example, the computer companies Bull and ICL both operate Total Care programmes.

WHAT TYPICALLY GOES WRONG?

With the growing sophistication of printers and personal computers, a lot of problems have arisen with the compatibility of configurations. And a common problem that occurs here is whether the printer has been set up properly. Indeed a common initial hurdle is software compatibility in setting up at the outset, coupled with lack of support from the dealer from whom the unit was purchased.

The advice is that you should get the dealer to set it up not just for you but for other member(s) of your staff. Can they work the equipment? Do they understand what to do? Do they know where the manuals are and how to refer to them? These may appear to be obvious points, but they are extremely important.

> The dealer should set it up not just for you but for other members of your staff - and everyone should be made aware of the features that the equipment offers

It is within the first 24 hours of purchase and ownership that major problems arise. The equipment may also be underutilised. Many features will not be used, in some cases because people weren't aware that they were there. People often spend money on features which they do not need.

PRINTER MAINTENANCE AND SERVICING

The computer is switched on. People are not familiar with this new addition. They get into a panic. Things aren't working, certainly not as they should be. They go to other people for advice or they ring the third party maintenance company. Enquiries for maintenance have to be filtered out. Third party maintenance companies receive a lot of calls from people having problems with their computers. Faults here can usually be rectified over the telephone. User training and questions of software compatibility can be given free, also over the telephone.

Once it has been established that the product is faulty, there are then certain common occurrences. Often paper will jam and all that is required are adjustments. A piece of plastic holding a key piece of the mechanics might snap. With dot matrix printers, there are lots of adjustments that can be required, eg cogs need to be unstuck, or springs need replacing.

If a printed circuit board should fail, it is usually an expensive part to replace. The comfort factor lies in the fact that PCBs on printers have similarly long life expectancies to those within computers.

In the area of laser printers, manufacturers say that the worst enemy is the user. There can be two reactions if the laser goes down: either the consumables have run out, but since it's a laser printer no-one wants to go near it; or it's treated the same as a photocopier, ie everyone fiddles with it or then someone says, 'What number do we ring for the copier repair man?'.

The laser printer is something different and special. The problems can vary, but the user guide, or maintenance advice and guidelines are often ignored. This leads to smudging and marks. So when the maintenance man is called out, the retort

112 PROFITING FROM YOUR PRINTER

is often 'It's your own fault so we're going to charge you'. One piece of advice is to get the maintenance man to teach you how to hoover out the inside of your laser, ie the little bits of carbon black, dust, paper dust, etc.

Then there are the ham-fisted types who always break things. Do not let them near the laser printer, particularly when the time comes round to change the unit's consumables. A gentle, caring approach will lead to a long and happy association.

> A gentle, caring approach to your laser printer will lead to a long and happy association

Some people are not suited to changing printer consumables

ICL'S VIEWS

Claiming to be the biggest computer-related operation in the UK, ICL's UK Customer Service division employs some 3,000 people. While all are involved in post sales support activities, there are 1,200 involved in pure traditional hardware engineering. Coverage is nationwide, plus extensions to both Northern and Southern Ireland, all off-shore islands and even oil rigs.

The largest number of breakdowns in any system, from personal computer through to mainframe, by far, occurs with the printer. Indeed the printer is viewed as the most vulnerable part of any configuration.

Problems will occur from human intervention, from not reading the manual properly or not being familiar with the system. Printers will break down most often because they have been undersold or underchosen.

All printers have a specified duty cycle. Many times, ICL has seen situations where a customer has been sold a low duty cycle machine, for example one designed to operate for two hours in any 24 hour period. The customer will then proceed to use the device as an output printer, churning out non-stop copy, and then become extremely aggravated when it fails.

The remedy here is that the people selling printers ought to understand the customer's requirements. The duty cycle must be ascertained and validated, which leads on to the cautionary advice that a cheap price gets a cheap solution.

> **The duty cycle must be ascertained and validated, which leads on to the cautionary advice that a cheap price gets a cheap solution**

ICL offers a service for all printers with the mission to meet all its customer requirements. The company bears in mind that the printer is one item of equipment that modern technology has not solved from the service point of view. The printer is still an electromechanical device.

Additionally, should a user be operating a system involving printers from three different manufacturers, ICL will still service all of the printers. Although the company sells many different types of printer, it is not a manufacturer of printers.

IBM'S CUSTOMER ENGINEERING ROLE

As befits the world's largest computer manufacturer, IBM has a support system which has been designed and developed along with the equipment, together with experience which IBM Customer Engineers (CEs) can draw upon, anywhere in the world. The standard IBM Maintenance Agreement gives you five day (Monday to Friday), 11 hour (8am to 7pm) cover. This can be extended to 18 or 24 hours, and there is provision for 11, 18 or 24 hour cover on Saturdays and Sundays too. Where applicable, the company will set up a preventative maintenance schedule tailored to your needs, and those of your system.

Some IBM cus..,ners make fewer than average calls on maintenance services, and so IBM has introduced its Retainer Service Agreement (RSA). Under this, customers can reduce service costs without losing the overall protection of the IBM Maintenance Agreement.

Under the RSA, IBM provides the same Customer Engineer support as that offered by the IBM Maintenance Agreement through a different price structure. A retainer fee covers all maintenance parts. When service is provided, labour is charged for at an appropriate hourly rate.

IBM has 15 hardware and two software centres strategically placed in the UK. If a user calls an IBM Branch Office with a problem, he or she will be asked to describe the symptoms. Having determined whether it's a hardware or software problem, access will then be made to the RETAIN diagnostic tool.

'Retain' (the IBM Remote Technical Assistance and Information Network) is an international communications network linked to a database containing the collected worldwide experience of its Customer Engineers, engineers and manufacturers. All IBM Customer Engineers have access to 'Retain' 24 hours a day, seven days a week. The database contains details of the description of the symptoms caused by the faults IBM has dealt with, plus how to cure them. Also included are the latest servicing techniques and tips.

IBM also offers a special on-site service for workstations called IBM Servicepoint. This is a fast, economic means of repairing IBM workstations. Instead of a new part, IBM exchanges the whole element.

In an office, the workstation is usually on the user's desk, as much a part of working life as the telephone. So if there's a problem, the last thing most people want is for an IBM Customer Engineer to use the desk as a workbench, dismantling your workstation and putting it back together.

IBM workstations are built in a modular style. Each product comprises separate functional elements like the keyboard, screen and printer

IBM workstations are built in a modular style. Each product comprises separate functional elements like the keyboard, screen and printer. Each element is transportable, and using simple diagnostic techniques, it's possible to identify which one has failed.

All that happens then is that you call a Customer Engineer and say which element is faulty. A courier brings an exchange module which can be substituted for the faulty one. The company also offers 'mail-in' or 'carry in' options, which are of course cheaper than the courier facility.

THE FOURTH PARTY

A facility which appears to be emerging now is the fourth party concept. At a time when printer units are becoming more transportable, in the ever-growing office markets, and demand is increasing for more central point repairing facilities, users will find themselves with two options.

They can parcel the printer up themselves and take it to the central repair site or they can have an engineer call. The engineer, however, will not often be asked to fix the unit; rather he or she will exchange the faulty unit for a replacement printer. Demand for this service is seen as emanating from offices, universities and third party companies.

The advantage for this approach, which encompasses a philosophy of opting for on-site or off-site service, is that downtime is zero - but you have to hold an extra printer in support. Then, while you are driving to the repair centre with the faulty unit, or an engineer is coming to pick it up, the replacement printer at your site can be up and running.

The savings - in suffering no downtime, having no loss of continuity and servicing your business' needs - more than compensate for the outlay on a spare printer. This particular approach has been pioneered by the company Sorbus, itself a major third party servicing, maintenance and repair operation.

The faulty unit is taken to the repair centre, where work can be done for other third party companies as well. One bonus point is that the customer has direct access to the repair facility.

HELPFUL BITS OF ADVICE
Backup

- Maintenance is not generally recognised at the low end of the printer spectrum. Indeed most maintenance companies countenancing a contract that will cover a low end machine - of the ilk of Citizen or Star printer for example - exclude the bits that go wrong, like the printhead. The Citizen and Star printers marketed with two years' warranty, for example, offer a warranty with the exclusion of the printhead.

A back-up machine or time-and-materials contract are considered better options than a maintenance contract. If you're spending below £500 (or in some quarters it's said to be £1,000) on a printer, it is not worth getting a maintenance contract. Maintenance on PCs and their systems is quite widely considered as 'money for old rope', the premise being that the electromechanical parts - like printers - are prone to malfunction.

Anyone with a large number of small and medium sized printers should carry a spare printer. It will pay handsome dividends.

Anyone with a large number of small and medium sized printers should carry a spare printer. It will pay handsome dividends

Throughput

- There are matrix printers around that 'go like rockets' and look on paper to be the answer to many Data Processing Managers' dreams. But if you're in the market for something really fast, the chances are that invariably you're going to need a printer that can handle proven high throughput rates. This is where many people have fallen down (along with their printer).

Cowboys

- Some companies use cheap labour to try and attain very low call out times, such as 24 hour call out. Often the call out will result in a part being needed - there's always an excuse. At one company, the engineer walked in, made a bee-line for the photocopier, looked at it and declared 'I believe this printer needs a part - I'll be back later'. The moral is: watch out for cowboys.

Copy clicks

- On maintenance contracts offered on laser printers, beware those involving copy clicks. People are trying to adopt the photocopier industry's practice whereby there's a minimum monthly contract of 6,000 copies (for example). What would you do if one month you only had 900 printouts? The engineer would reset the counter on his regular visit. Look out for this.

Small Print

- Shortly after setting up a printer, an early maintenance call out is generally made for user errors, minor teething problems, etc. But do watch out for the small print on your contract - of what's not included in the maintenance contract, like print bands, shuttle modules, etc. These can set you back £300-£400 a time.

> Watch out for the small print on your contract - of what's not included in the maintenance contract, like print bands, shuttle modules, etc. These can set you back £300-£400 a time

Maintenance

- Whichever printer you get, make sure that a reliable company is maintaining the product.

The higher up the printer spectrum one goes, the more complex becomes the product. And the greater the need to have full confidence that you have the best possible maintenance arrangements. Because of their nature, printers are system components and play a major part in computer processing. The products should be supported by a company with both able technicians and a large stock of spare parts.

CHAPTER 8

THE DIFFERENT TYPES OF PRINTER

PRINTERS: TRENDS AND DEVELOPMENTS

The printer market is in a state of flux, particularly at the lower ends where non-impact technologies are beginning to challenge the dominance of the dot matrix machines. During the 1990s we can expect to see a gradual shift in emphasis away from the impact devices to the non-impact technologies of laser (of whatever type), ink jet (all types) and thermal transfer.

PRINTER MARKETS

The value of the total market for printers in Europe - that's from the big machines down to 9-pin dot matrix printers - is estimated to be about $2.5 billion for 1989 (according to a variety of sources but including Romtec and IDC). The value of the computer market as a whole in Europe in 1989 was estimated to have been some $50 billion.

Worldwide sales of printers (in numbers of units) in 1988 were estimated at 2.45 million, up from 2.16 million the previous year. According to IDC and Dataquest, the years to 1992 will see a radical shift of market shares in the individual market segments of the European printer market.

The market share of impact printers is expected to decrease by over 6 per cent per year while serial printers are expected to rise by nearly 1.5 per cent. Page printers (in particular laser printers) are expected to rise by over 35 per cent.

OFFICE PRINTERS: TECHNOLOGY AND MARKETS

The value of the European office printer market is probably about $1.4 billion, and the bulk of this is made up of dot matrix, thermal transfer, ink jet, daisywheel, laser, light emitting diode and liquid crystal shutter technology printers.

Looking around a typical office, the chances are that you will find letters being pumped out on daisywheel devices - even typewriters - and invoices clattering out of matrix printers. Despite these first impressions, however, there is a trend away from these long-established impact technologies towards the non-impact laser (including LEDs and LCDs), inkjet and thermal transfer technologies.

> There is a trend away from these long established impact technologies towards the non-impact laser (including LEDs and LCDs), inkjet and thermal transfer technologies

Disadvantages of non-impact technologies are mainly the high cost of the consumables (toner cartridges, etc) and their inability to handle multi-part forms printing. They offer considerable advantages and flexibility in other areas, however, particularly with print quality and low noise.

LASER PRINTERS: TECHNOLOGY AND MARKETS

Laser printers have experienced phenomenal growth over the past four years or so, and they now account for about 15 per cent of all printer sales. However, the cost of laser printers is still high compared to other types of printer: the 15 per cent of sales accounts for about 45 per cent of the market in value.

Seven vendors shared 87 per cent of all laser printer unit sales. Hewlett-Packard was in first position with 44 per cent unit share (and a slightly lower 39 per cent value share). Apple took second place with a 14 per cent share, followed by Canon with 10 per cent. Next was Brother (6 per cent), Kyocera (5 per cent), Epson (5 per cent) and Apricot (3 per cent).

Laser printers have experienced phenomenal growth over the past four years or so, and they now account for about 15 per cent of all printer sales. However, the cost of laser printers is still high compared to other types of printer

LASER PRINTERS: PRODUCTS

These fall into two broad categories: office lasers or PostScript lasers for desktop publishing applications. PostScript is the de facto industry standard page description language being supported by the likes of Apple, Digital, Wang and IBM.

The clear choice for the PostScript page description language camp is the Apple Laserwriter IINTX which has a list price of around £4500. The Apple machine, as with many others, is based on a Canon engine which offers superb print quality and also Hewlett-Packard LaserJet II emulation, making it suitable for non-PostScript applications.

In the office category the top slot goes to the Hewlett-Packard LaserJet Series II, which has a list price of around £2000, and the Series IID, which has a list price of around £3000. These are both based around the Canon SX engine, used in 80 per cent of laser beam printers worldwide.

However, fresh on to the market now is Canon's LBP-8 Mark III laser which has a list price of around £2000 and, most

THE DIFFERENT TYPES OF PRINTER 125

importantly, will not be available through anyone other than Canon.

The device offers a combination of scalable fonts and high speed graphics and is aimed fairly and squarely at desktop publishing and wordprocessing users. Scalable means you can choose a typeface and enlarge it or reduce it to literally any point size you like without changing cartridges and without downloading.

Aside from the Hewlett-Packard LaserJet and the Canon machine, there are other laser printers which are considered worthy enough to be recommended. Everyone these days seems to be marketing a laser printer. It's definitely the vogue. Apple, Brother, Olivetti and Star market their own variety of the Canon engine which will invariably be compared with the Hewlett-Packard LaserJet, sometimes quite rightly. Inevitably, the HP machine wins.

Kyocera, Panasonic and Toshiba make their own engines and the results are often the same as those extolled in the previous paragraph. But they all try to pack more features in than anyone else. The engine in Dataproduct's laser is from Toshiba and that in Mannesmann Tally's is from Kyocera, for example. Citizen uses a Sharp engine in its Overture 106 laser printer which prints at 6 pages per minute, and which is said to be one of the smallest units around. Citizen uses Mita manufactured engines for its larger 110 and 112 laser printers.

Other manufacturers of laser engines include Ricoh (which provides the engines for IBM, Epson and Oki laser printers for example) and Hitachi (which includes Qume among its customers). By all accounts it's a busy marketplace and the lion's share is held by the Canon engine.

An interesting development, not strictly a laser printer is Qume's CrystalPrint Series II, which is a six pages per minute unit based on liquid crystal shutter technology housed in an engine made by Casio. Actually, the Crystalprint is not a laser printer although it uses a very similar technology. Its light source is a fluorescent light which shines through an array of liquid crystals. These flicker on and off to selectively shut off the light from the photosensitive drum rotating through the beam.

Despite the claimed advantages of light emitting diode (LED) and liquid crystal shutter (LCS) printers over traditional laser engines, LED and LCS printers comprised only about 1 per cent of the laser market in 1988.

MATRIX PRINTERS: TECHNOLOGY AND MARKETS

Although the trend is moving towards laser printers, the most common printer technology in use today is still dot matrix. Most popular, with some 50 per cent of total office equipment printer sales, are the 9-pin printers. These are also the cheapest printers on the market.

> Although the trend is moving towards laser printers, the most common printer technology in use today is still dot matrix

However, there is vigorous growth in the 18 and 24-pin matrix printers, and, according to Romtec, these now account for about a quarter of dot matrix printers sales.

The more pins there are in the printhead of an impact dot matrix printer, the better the quality of output. The printhead moves across the page and forms characters by striking a ribbon with a different sequence of pins for each character. Colour printing is possible with multi-coloured print ribbons and the results are quite tolerable.

Recognising the wide variety of matrix printers, they are here divided for convenience into the following categories: top-of-the-line 24-pin machines; upmarket 9 and 18-pin machines; mid-price 24-pin units; mid-price 9 and 18-pin units; low-cost 24-pin machines; and low-cost 9 and 18-pin units.

TOP-END 24-PIN MATRIX PRINTERS

The IBM 5204 Quickwriter has been well-received; priced at around £1,250, it is made in Italy. The device has a draft speed of 333 characters per second (at 10 characters per inch), boasts a full range of paper-handling functions and options, and offers a carbon ribbon for better output. It is probably equalled in print quality only by NEC's 24-pin output. (For information about draft and near letter quality output from printers, *see* page 6).

Competitors to IBM's Quickwriter include Epson's LQ-2550, which has similar speeds, and Fujitsu's DL5600, which a rated draft speed (at 10 characters per inch) of 405 characters per second. Both boast colour capability as standard, and have many resident fonts.

Slightly cheaper is the Oki Microline 393C, listed at £1,195 for a 300 characters per second unit, also with colour.

UPMARKET 9 AND 18-PIN MATRIX PRINTERS

These are generally of Japanese origin. Of the machines in this sector several can be highlighted - for example, Seikosha's SBP-10AI which is an 18-pin device weighing in at 33kg, priced at around £3000, and offering a draft speed (at 10 characters per inch) of 800 characters per second. Its main applications are expected to lie in the heavy duty line printer area of minis and some mainframes. List price is £2,999.

The Brother M-4018, which costs around £1500, prints at 400 characters per second at 10 characters per inch in draft mode. This machine is outperformed on throughput only by some of the more expensive machines.

> The main applications of upmarket 9 and 18-pin matrix printers are expected to lie in the heavy duty line printer area of minis and some mainframes

There is also the Epson DFX-5000 9-pin heavyweight (29kg) at around £1700 which operates with twin feed continuous stationery over a split platen at speeds of up to 533 characters per second. Its main application is seen as a high volume terminal printer on local area network servers.

MID-PRICE 24-PIN PRINTERS

NEC has maintained a consistent presence in this market sector. Universal acclaim goes to its P-6 Plus printer which costs around £650 and operates at 220 characters per second at 10 characters per inch in draft mode. It is regarded as good value for the £649 price tag, with excellent quality print.

Other good quality machines include the Epson LQ-850, Citizen ProDot 24, Fujitsu DL3300 and 3400 (also sold by Olivetti as the DM 250 and 250 L, but at lower prices), IBM Proprinter X24 and XL24 and Oki Microline 390 and 391. Despite other manufacturers' models having some advantages (for example, IBM's unit features a lower list price than the P6 Plus), the edge is still given over to NEC.

MID-PRICE 9 AND 18-PIN PRINTERS

The period 1988/9 has seen the introduction of some outstanding new devices into this sector. Top of the pile of the 9-pin crop is the Oki Microline 320, and the wide carriage version the 321. List prices are £525 and £675 respectively, with draft speeds of 300 characters per second at 10 characters per inch.

The throughput of these devices is considered to be good as a result of combining the high print speed with an efficient paper-handling system. Printers which beat these units in throughput tests are usually in the £1,500 to £3,000 range.

Other worthy printers for this category are the IBM Proprinter III and III XL, Epson FX-850 and FX-1050, Brother M-2518, Seikosha MP-1300AI and MP-5300AI, and Citizen Prodot 9/9x series.

LOW COST 24-PIN MATRIX PRINTERS

A significant product in this category is Epson's LQ-500 which rates 150 characters per second at 10 characters per inch, and costs about £400. It is well supported by software packages and its print quality is good. Widely regarded as an all-rounder.

Other good value devices around this price are the NEC P2200 and Star's LC24-10, as well as Citizen's Swift-24, which rates 160 characters per second.

LOW COST 9 AND 18-PIN MATRIX PRINTERS

This is the domain of the low volume applications world, of invoices, etc, where appearance is not the highest priority. What's needed are good, basic machines that offer a reasonable number of functions in a reasonably efficient manner for a reasonable amount of money. Highly regarded is the Star LC-10 9-pin machine. Other mentions are usually made of Amstrad, Brother and Panasonic.

DAISYWHEEL PRINTERS

The daisywheel printer has suffered from the laser printer's success. Few daisywheel printers are marketed today (their market share is 4 per cent). Moreover, daisywheel printers cost almost as much as laser printers, which demands considerable commitment from prospective purchasers.

DAISYWHEEL PRINTERS: PRODUCTS

Now in the twilight zone of its existence, daisywheel technology has had its day, and awaits the final squeezing into oblivion from the rapidly growing laser markets and fast-emerging inkjet fraternity.

> Daisywheel technology has had its day, and awaits the final squeezing into oblivion from the growing laser and inkjet markets

Daisywheels are noisy, most work at speeds up to 40 characters per second and can cost anything up to £1,000 (eg, the recommended Brother HR-40 is listed at £995). They are not very versatile; they cannot do a graphics printout, for example. In addition, a sheet feeder is often required for letter quality work which demands work with cut sheets.

In their favour, however, daisywheel printers do produce the best letter quality around (although even that statement is fast becoming suspect) and they are reliable, which counts for a lot these days. They are also good for multi-part forms.

INKJET PRINTERS: TECHNOLOGY AND MARKETS

The inkjet printer, or rather the new range of inkjet printers, is already sounding the death knell for the daisywheel printer. According to Romtec, the inkjet market showed the greater unit and value growth in 1988, of 128 per cent and 135 per cent respectively.

> Inkjet printers cost little more than matrix printers and offer outputs that approach and sometimes surpass those of laser printers, for a fraction of the price of a laser

Seven vendors accounted for 91 per cent of unit sales - including IBM (now withdrawn from this market). Hewlett-Packard's four inkjet models accounted for 48 per cent of unit sales while Epson's one model accounted for 13 per cent of unit sales and 23 per cent of sales value.

Both Canon (8 per cent) and Siemens (7 per cent) have long been associated with the inkjet market, while Integrex (4 per cent) rebadges a Canon unit. Sales of Diconix's portable range of inkjet printers resulted in a 5 per cent unit share.

Inkjet printers have overcome the problems of clogged-up jets and messy ink reproduction that have beset them for so long, and are indeed set to rise from the current 5 per cent market share to assume a significant presence. They cost little more than matrix printers and offer outputs that approach and sometimes surpass those of laser printers, for a fraction of the price of a laser. On the downside, the cost of inkjet consumables is high, and, as is normal for any new technology, there is no track record of reliability to fall back on for reference.

INKJET PRINTERS: PRODUCTS

As this is very much an emerging product line, there are not many inkjet devices on the market. A significant machine, at around £800, for low volume letter quality applications, is the Hewlett-Packard DeskJet. The device shares a common technology with the Canon BJ-130 'bubble jet' printer.

However, although the output from these printers is considered to be better than that from a laser it does not mean that it is better for you to opt for ink jet, if only for the fact that the cost of consumables is higher. The speed is also somewhat less.

The only problems with this technology is that while it produces output of a quality comparable to a laser and is as quiet as a laser, it lacks the versatility of a laser

Another interesting product is the Dataproducts SI 480 printer which uses solid ink pellets. These are melted on to the page to produce outstanding print quality.

The only problems with this technology in the current market is that while it produces output of a quality comparable to a laser and daisywheel text, and in operation it's as quiet as a laser, it lacks the versatility of a laser. In sum, from the three models detailed here, there are undoubtedly applications in the text/letter quality camps where these devices score hands down over any laser or daisywheel.

THERMAL TRANSFER PRINTERS

The other new development is the thermal transfer printer, currently with a 5 per cent market share. These printers produce excellent quality output at speeds ranging from 80 to 300 characters per second, even in colour for which the technology is rated at being very good. Drawbacks are the high costs of ownership (the ribbons are very expensive) and the need for a sheet feeder for cut sheet applications.

In operation a thermal transfer printer can cost you up to 10p per page and the printhead apparently needs replacing quite often. The good news is that these costs are expected to come down - the only question is when.

LINE PRINTERS: TECHNOLOGY

Line printers are not for general office use, but for high speed bulk printing, for example in a data-processing department.

Line printing is the generic term for two fundamentally different kinds of technology, which are both intended for applications where the critical factors are speed and reliability rather than quality of presentation: band printers and line matrix printers.

BANDPRINT

The oldest and still thriving technology is band printing, where a steel band embossed with 48, 64 or 96 alphanumeric characters produces characters on paper on a line-by-line basis. Having been around for some 12 years, the technology lacks sophistication, but offers unassailable high speed.

Hitachi, for example, offers a unit which works at speeds of up to 2,000 lines per minute.

LINE MATRIX PRINTING

Line matrix printers are more sophisticated and flexible than band printers, but work at lower speeds. A horizontal array of 24 print hammers fitted on a shuttle, which strike simultaneously, print a whole line of dots in one sweep. When the sweep is completed, the printer advances the paper one dot row, changes the shuttle direction and prints the next row.

Line matrix printers can also offer graphics, even high resolution graphics on some models in several formats, including line drawing and block graphics, plotting and bar codes. In addition, line printers usually provide a greater choice of facilities such as superscript and subscript, bold type, etc, with some machines able to mix text, graphics and character pitch in the same print line.

> Line printing technology is reliable, yet static and has probably advanced technologically as far as it will go. Over the past few years, annual revenues in the line matrix and band printer sectors has been flat

Line printing technology is reliable, yet static and has probably advanced technologically as far as it will go. Over the past few years, annual revenues in these two line printer sectors have been flat, standing at about $650 million for band printers and nearly $400 million for line matrix printers.

LINE PRINTERS: MARKETS

Line printers, in contrast to daisywheel and dot matrix printers, are not particularly vulnerable to attack from non-impact printers, especially laser printers.

One reason is that line printer applications do not demand high quality output, and there is little obvious need in data processing departments for the high print quality provided by laser printers.

Line printers are not vulnerable to attack from non-impact printers as their applications do not demand high quality output

The situation is different for the bulk of laser printer applications, such as letter-writing or desktop publishing, where the prime requirement is quality. Until now these high quality applications have been performed by daisywheel and dot matrix printers, and, indeed, the typewriter.

Other important defences against a laser printer incursion are speed, price and running costs.

A laser outputting 40 pages a minute is roughly equivalent to a line printer output of 2,000 lines per minute (laser printer performance is usually measured using A4 size paper while that of line printers by using 130 column fanfold paper). Not many laser printers can perform at this rate. Indeed, laser printers currently cluster, either at the low end, around the 10 pages per minute level or, at the top end, around 100 pages per minute. Pricing is also a key factor. A quality line matrix printer will cost about £10,000 while a top end laser printer will cost about £100,000, leaving it very much in the domain of top users such as banks and building societies.

Cost of ownership is another important factor. A band printer will cost about 0.1p per sheet to throughput while a 20 pages per minute laser printer will cost 3p per sheet. This calculation does not include the paper. Over a five year period a laser printer could cost around £2,300 in toner cartridges.

Line matrix printers are also good at barcoding and labelling, which is a boon today with more and more companies opting to do this work themselves instead of sending it out to third parties.

Looking ahead to 1993, however, the consensus is that line matrix printer revenues are likely to fall while the band printer level is expected to hold reasonably steady.

Band printers, working at 600 lines per minute and above, are resistant to other technologies because there is little that can compete, either in price or reliability.

However, line matrix printers, which start at 300 lines per minute, are vulnerable to dot matrix technology. Many dot matrix printers today offer similar speeds, but with the added advantage of much improved graphics capability. Despite this, it is likely that many users will stay with the tried and tested technology of line matrix technology, as it provides multi-part form printing as well as high operating speeds.

Refer to Chapter 9 for suggestions, referrals and reviews of particular printers for defined applications.

CHAPTER 9

WHICH PRINTER FOR A PARTICULAR APPLICATION?

There is no one printer that is good for each and every application. Such a machine does not exist. This chapter will list equipment that has a proven pedigree, is universally known to be highly rated, or is otherwise judged to be worthy of inclusion. Benchmarks run by independent parties have been used wherever possible to determine a placing.

Read this chapter bearing in mind that the figures quoted reflect 1989 pricing structures and inflation. Remember that prices and costs which have been included are for guidance only and should not be taken as being the precise figures at which those machines are available today. However, these figures will give you useful guidance as to the sort of prices you may be asked to pay.

Generally, list prices will be quoted together with an idea of what sort of discounted price may be obtained; for example, you should be able to negotiate at least 25 per cent off a one-off purchase. The same goes for supplies and consumables. And you don't just have to go to the printer manufacturer for these either, because there are lots of third party suppliers - all flogging the same stuff at much more competitive rates.

Generally list prices will be quoted together with an idea of what sort of discounted price may be obtained: for example, you should be able to negotiate at least 25 per cent off a one-off purchase

The pricing trend for matrix printers is upwards however, due in no short measure to the effect of EEC levies imposed as a result of anti-dumping action against the Japanese printer manufacturers.

If you find yourself in a bargaining position, make sure the discount you're being offered applies to all the options you've decided to take as well. It's no good getting your printer for

WHICH PRINTER FOR A PARTICULAR APPLICATION? 139

£500, say, if you've then got to pay £600 for a dual bin sheet feeder and £200 for an envelope feeder.

Make sure the discount applies across all the extras. Make sure, too, that you've agreed a price for consumables (although a ribbon or set of laser supplies, etc, should be included anyway), and don't forget your paper.

The section will start with 9-pin dot matrix printers and move progressively upwards through different ranges of printers.

The number of printers on the market today poses a great problem for the software houses as writing programs for printer drivers is expensive. With so many printers on the market, it is difficult to know which ones to support.

It's no better, either, looking at the matter from the other side of the fence, ie from the manufacturers' point of view. To support all the applications on the market would mean paying programmers to produce myriad versions of the software, which would be prohibitely expensive.

A universal graphics printer-driver standards is needed so that the manufacturers only have one driver to write and the software houses only one printer specification to support

What's called for is a universal graphics printer-driver standard so that the manufacturers only have one driver to write and the software houses only one printer specification to support.

However, such a standard does exist. Known as the ANSI/ISO DP9636, it defines the computer-graphics interface (CGI) structure for driving printers, display adapters and plotters. A file structure for transferring pictures as metafiles is also specified. Implementing these standards would solve most of the problems related to printer incompatibilities.

Many applications today already use the standard, but most of the popular application programs do not. To assist, many device drivers already exist.

These cover all sorts of equipment, including development toolkits and linkages to the frontrunners of the compilers.

So, when buying your printer, check that it offers all its features for the graphics packages it supports. Some printer drivers do not use the highest resolution of the printer. You will have to watch this point, because if it's stated that support for a family of printers is offered, it could be that only those features found on the most basic model in the range are supported.

> **When buying your printer, check that it offers all its features for the graphics packages it supports**

Ensure that all your printer's features are maintained when it is operating in its emulation mode. But before you part with any money, ask to see how the printer handles output from the applications you have in mind.

9-PIN DOT MATRIX PRINTERS

Pins are arranged in a single vertical row in nine pin print heads. The print head is mounted on a track so that it can slide back and forth across the paper surface. A character is formed on the paper by colouring an appropriate pattern of spots with a so-called character box of horizontal and vertical spot positions in a rectangular matrix pattern.

The number of positions in the character box depends on the resolution of the printer.

As the head slides on its track, each pin required to form a vertical slice of the character or graphic is fired by releasing the electromagnet that holds it back from the ribbon. A microprocessor within the printer controls which pins are released, as well as where they are released during the print head's run across the track.

Once, 9-pin dot matrix printers were just not capable of letter quality printing. The first attempts at improving letter quality resulted in the units having the ability to emphasise characters by printing extra dots vertically, horizontally or both at once. This technique did admittedly give a likeness to true printing, but the results were not really what you would call quality.

Today nearly all 9-pin matrix printers offer near letter quality (NLQ) fonts. Many of these are suitable for company correspondence, and certainly all home users should be more than satisfied. A noble and true domain of course is for invoicing and general accounts work. Other than this, high volume draft printing is a perfect domain for nine pins.

Nowadays, changing forms is a pleasure rather than a task. Many of the new printers offer the user the choice of inserting paper from the front, back or bottom. Some even have an output tray that holds the printed paper away from paper still being fed in (and anyone who's experienced a paper jam on a printer that doesn't have these facilities will know what a boon that is).

Other printers have built-in stands that give you a place beneath the printer for input and output paper. Some printers load your paper automatically. You push the end of your stack of paper into a slot, press a button and the unit's tractor takes over.

Perforated paper, of whatever quality, that's been passed through a printer will always obviously be 'perforated' even if you manage to strip the holy bits of paper from the paper afterwards. Company images can fold flat with a mismanaged print out.

So today, to get round this one, you can stick sheet feeders to many of the new breed of matrix printers. Put in your letter headed notepaper, or you may be fortunate to have multiple bins to feed in continuation sheets (but watch out for the software).

So if it's nine pin for you, what's likely to be a good buy?

Cheap/low price 9-pin

The Star LC-10 is generally accorded a leading position. Also available with a colour option, the units list for £259 and £299 respectively but you can buy them for about £175 and £200. Some resident fonts are offered plus emulations of Epson devices and the IBM Proprinter standard.

Brother M-1209, listed at £265 but possible to be bought for £190, offers emulations of Epson FX-1000 and IBM Proprinter standard. Competes hotly with the Star unit. A cheaper machine is the Panasonic KX-P1081 which is listed at £219 but can be bought for less than £150. It offers Epson RX-80, IBM Graphics Printer and Proprinter standard, and is viewed as rugged and good value.

Medium price 9-pin

Universal acclaim is a byword for the Oki Microline 320 and

Microline 321 devices (80 columns and 136 columns respectively). Capable of high volume draft printing, they're list priced at £525 and £675 respectively, although it's possible to get them for less than £400 and about £500 respectively. Emulations of Epson FX printers and the IBM Proprinter are offered.

Epson has come out with new versions of its bestselling FX printer range. Lists are £459 for the FX-850 (80 column) and £599 for the FX-1050 (136 column) while it's possible to get these machines for much, much less - just over £300 and £400 respectively. They are good nine pin machines, but surpassed on throughput by the Oki models.

IBM's 4201 Proprinter III and 4202 Proprinter III XL devices display a laudable performance. Similarly priced to the Epson machines, they're not renowned for high volume applications but have an excellent draft throughput.

Another range tucking in behind the Oki units comes from Seikosha. The MP-1300AI and MP-5300AI sell for similar prices to the above and display good throughputs for draft printing. Citizen's ProDot 9 and 9X (list price £439 and £559 respectively) offer 300 characters per inch (at 12 dots per inch) and 60 characters per second at 10 dots per inch.

Upmarket 9-pin

The only one worth mentioning is the Epson DFX-5000, which has a 300 characters per second high speed draft mode of operation. This machine offers both front and rear feed tractors and a smooth means of switching between them. It's listed at £1,699 but can be got for about £1,200. It should be considered particularly for networking applications as the printer on a file server.

18-PIN DOT MATRIX PRINTERS

Print quality has never been too much of a problem with 18-pin printers.

From the outset these machines were designed to stand up against daisywheel printers and take over the letter quality market. Effectively, these offer you a 9-pin quality but at an improved speed, making them good choices for draft applications, for example. But although esigned to produce good quality output, it is not advisable to buy 18-pin printers for near letter quality. This is because, with the pricing and discounting available now, you are much better off opting for 24-pin devices.

Medium price 18-pin

The Brother M-2518 represents good value here. Optimised for rugged office environments where thick multi-part forms and volume printing are the norm, this unit features a patented system for paper handling called Paper Express. Unlike traditional rear-feed paper mechanisms which feed paper at a 90 degree angle around the platen, this printer's mechanism feeds paper at a 45 degree angle (like a photocopier or laser printer). The concept is that a straight, short, flat paper path offers the maximum print head impact. It also has a self-adjusting printhead. List price is £895 but it's possible to get one for about £660 if you shop around.

Upmarket 18-pin

Given the opening remarks to this section, it would be surprising to see an upmarket machine recommended.

However, worthy of mention are the Brother M-4018 and Seikosha SBP-10.

The former retails at a hefty £1,495 but you can get it for just over £1,000. The unit shows a good throughput rate with commendable paper-handling facilities. Colour is standard and draft speed of operation is 400 characters per second. It's said to be good for 'heavy' stationery such as multi-part forms and labels.

The Seikosha SBP-10AI is a large 33kg machine that produces good quality type at terrific speeds (800 characters per second at 10 characters per inch in draft mode) which is ideal for users needing to produce a lot of spreadsheets. The other side of this coin is that its very high price (listed at about £3,000, but you should be able to get it for about £2,200) could make you consider buying something else. It's as fast as a laser, offers much greater paper-handling flexibility, costs less than 0.5p per page, deals with greater volumes and also handles A3 size paper. But you should only really consider this if you have high volume print runs.

Mannesmann Tally's 340 is ideally suited for heavy use too, in large offices. Definitely not intended for single users either (it costs just under £1,500), it is rugged and operates at 190 characters per second. It should suit applications where large quantities of good quality type are needed, and where these considerations outweigh the inconvenience of changing printer settings.

24-PIN DOT MATRIX PRINTERS

These machines are poor choices if all you want to do is produce draft work. If that's all you want to do, you're much better off with an 18-pin printer. They're cheaper and they also do the job just as quickly. The 24-pin device is in the premier league if some of your work involves NLQ printing and you also need to switch between NLQ and draft modes.

Cheap/low price 24-pin

Significant in this category is the Epson LQ-500. Its plus points are that it's well supported by software packages and the print quality is excellent; throughput is good and performance good for the price (under £400 on list or about £275 if you shop around). The machine does lack many of the features you might expect from your printer though. It has an awkward paper feed system and there's lack of support for envelope and label printing, which could prove a limitation. It is inexpensive, however, and would make a good back-up machine. If you've opted for 24-pin and this is your budget, go for it, but if your budget stretches up by another hundred it might pay to look around.

The NEC Pinwriter P2200 was the machine which introduced the sub-£400 24-pin letter quality printer category back in 1987. It's a compact and inexpensive (£395 say at list or £275 if you look around) machine which offers slow yet excellent letter quality printing (75 characters per second at 10 characters per inch). The machine does lack NEC's build quality as it has been manufactured within strict cost budgets. If you are on a tight budget and have a low volume requirement, this is for you. If your budget is higher and you are pro-NEC take a look at the P6 Plus and P7 Plus.

The Star LC24-10 is considered a solid contender in this highly-competitive sector. It has a lot to offer for the price (similar to the previous two) but is a bit loud (ranging from 77dB to 71dB) and a bit slow (142 characters per second in draft mode at 10 characters per inch). It offers a pleasing range of typefaces, many variations on print styles (eg outline and shadow print) and many emulations.

Citizen's Swift-64 (list price £389) offers 160 characters per second in draft mode at 10 characters per inch (192 at 12 characters per inch) or 53 characters per second at near letter quality at 10 characters per inch (64 at 12 characters per inch). Noise level is rated at 55dB.

Medium price 24-pin

Without hesitation, the coveted place in this competitive band goes to NEC's P6 Plus and P7 Plus (listed at under £650 and £840 respectively, and targetted at about £450 and £570 respectively). In the busy 24-pin market, you really do have to decide which features you want most on your printer.

> In the busy 24-pin market, you really do have to decide which features you want most on your printer

In this case, your range of choices includes impressive font choices, 80k input buffer, good printing speed (220 characters per second in draft mode at 10 characters per inch, 75 characters per second in letter quality mode) and a quoted mean time between failures figure of 6,000 hours. However, the P6 Plus is really a more sophisticated and faster version than NEC's 2200 machine - a cheap 24-pin job (£395 list) that produces good letter quality output. The question to ask yourself, given the output of the more expensive version, is whether it's worth the extra money.

Fujitsu sell some excellent mid-price 24-pin machines in the shape of the DL3300 and DL3400 (wide and narrow carriage as before). List prices are £710 and £825 respectively, while it's possible to get them for under £500 and about £550 respectively. There are impressive options such as font expansion capabilities and colour, while draft speed at 10 characters per inch is 240 characters per second and (very good) NLQ speed is 60 characters per second. They are good but acknowledged to be beaten in a price/performance comparison by NEC's P6 Plus and P7 Plus.

Olivetti also sells the Fujitsu DL3300 and DL3400 units but as the DM 250/250 L. While they are cheaper through Olivetti, there's no guarantee that you're going to get trouble-free operation - there is no 24-pin emulation so you will have to use a Fujitsu printer driver if you want to avoid having to operate the machine with the 9-pin IBM Graphics Printer emulation that is offered as standard. It might be worth your while spending a bit more money on buying the Fujitsu originals.

You cannot ignore IBM in the computer scene, and in the mid-price area the company sells its 4207 Proprinter X24 and 4208 Proprinter XL24 devices which produce sharp text and graphics at speeds of 240 characters per second in draft mode and 80 characters per second in NLQ mode. These are solid machines and good value.

Just cheaper than NEC's P6 Plus and P7 Plus (list £599 and £789, targets about £450 and £585), the Oki Microline 390 and 391 offer crisp and speedy text output in both Epson LQ-1500 and IBM Proprinter emulations with a 'friendly' user interface. Both printers offer three emulations, one of which is compatible with the Proprinter Alternate Graphics Mode, plus six typefaces and full front panel control. They also come with a 23k buffer, half of which can be devoted to downloaded fonts. Citizen's ProDot 24, (list £599) has 200 characters per second draft speed with 24k buffer. All this power and flexibility can be accessed easily, and these are printers to be viewed as all-purpose printers.

Upmarket 24-pin

This is the domain of machines costing well over £1,000 and as such must be intended for specialised applications.

Don't bother looking at 24-pin machines if all you want is a printer to churn out spreadsheets or perform invoicing or low level work. Remember too that for letter quality work on a matrix printer, you will need to buy a sheet feeder. Also, you're now in laser land, regarding purchase cost, so you must be aware of your applications' needs.

> Don't bother looking at 24-pin machines if all you want is a printer to churn out spreadsheets or perform invoicing or low level work

IBM's 5204 Quickwriter is very fast - 330 characters per second in draft mode at 10 characters per inch and 110 characters per second in NLQ mode.

Furthermore, the machine delivers excellent print and comes with a range of optional paper handling devices and fonts that are hard, if not impossible to beat. In fact the only print quality to exceed this comes from NEC's 24-pin print. Basic list price is £1,253 while it's possible to obtain one for about £940.

However, you will probably want to add the tractor feed, 32k buffer, both sheet feeder options and some font cartridges. This will add at least £900 or so. But you will get a near unbeatable system, that will suit volume quality printing applications, including letters and envelopes.

Fujitsu's DL5600 costs just as much as a laser (list £1,850 but it's possible to obtain one for about £1,250) but does deliver everything you could possibly want from a dot matrix printer.

Draft speeds at 10 characters per inch are 405 characters per second while NLQ speeds are 135 characters per second. Consequently, it offers a good draft and NLQ throughput combination which is surpassed on draft speeds only by some heavy duty machines. The DL5600 offers emulations of Diablo 630, Epson FX-80 and JX-80, IBM Graphics Printer and IBM Proprinter XL, plus four good resident fonts. You can also set the machine up for a variety of uses, including colour printing. The DL5600 is fast enough for multiple users and versatile enough for most applications.

The Epson LQ-2550 is by far the best of the company's offerings in the 24-pin camp. Already the LQ series has set a very high standard for 24-pin print quality and this printer is Epson's best letter quality printer yet.

There are seven resident fonts (more than most people will ever use); it's also a colour printer, and there's an easy-to-use control panel. List prices is £1,299 but shop around and it should be possible to buy one for just over £900. Draft speeds at 10 characters per inch are 330 characters per second, and NLQ speeds are 110 characters per second.

Continuous form paper up to 16 inch wide can be used with the LQ-2550 and you can select between tractor, friction or single sheet feed directly from the front control panel. The built-in tractor feed is of the push type but an external pull tractor option is offered. Another option is a dual bin cut sheet feeder that holds 150 sheets of paper per bin. The only emulation is Epson LQ standard. This printer is considered a reliable workhorse for the office, producing printed material with which you would never be ashamed to be associated.

The Oki Microline 393C maintains Oki's reputation for sharp output with an extra bonus of colour capability. As such it is suitable for all types of work except professional desk top publishing jobs. List price is £1,195 while it's possible to obtain one for about £900. Draft speed at 10 characters per inch is 300 characters per second and NLQ is 100 characters per second. The printer has the Courier typeface resident. There is a font cartridge bay for your choice of Prestige or Gothic, and typefaces can appear in five pitches. Buffer space is between 8k and 30k depending on the use of font cartridges. You can design your own downloadable characters, but it is not possible to buy any from Oki. All the versatility you could need is probably contained in this unit.

The Toshiba P351SX is another wide carriage 24-pin device. List price is £1,099 with a target level of £750. A front panel options menu and paper parking facility make it easy to use, but the only emulations offered do not include a 24-pin emulation. Toshiba's market presence, however, means that special printer drivers within software packages will most likely be available to overcome that potential problem.

LASER PRINTERS

There are basically two types of market for laser printers: there are the office lasers and PostScript lasers. Debate has been rife that personal laser printers would soon be a new market. This particular class of product would break the £700 price tag, allowing laser printers to begin displacing dot matrix printers in large quantities while simultaneously eliminating 'laser envy'. A level of personal non-impact printers has been identified whose parameters include a below 5 pages per minute rating and a typical end user price of under £700.

> There are basically two types of market for laser printers: there are the office lasers and Postscript lasers. Debate has been rife that personal laser printers would soon be a new market

As of early 1990, no laser printer fits that description, but non-laser products do, such as the Hewlett-Packard Deskjet and Canon BJ130 ink jet printers. Laser print engine prices are not expected to decrease, if only because of the dollar/yen relationship. Even if print engine prices could be brought down, a less than £700 laser printer would require a limited controller, probably with a single emulation and little memory.

At least two companies are known to be working on low end laser printers but both have had print quality problems, and quality will be a key factor that undoubtedly could inhibit sales.

It is generally thought that the personal page printer market could be satisfied by 3 to 4 pages per minute devices. For example, for a large corporate with say 100 desks, it would be possible to configure each page printer identically with the one emulation.

In 1988, eight pages per minute laser printers based on the Canon engine and exemplified by the Hewlett-Packard Laserjet dominated the laser market, accounting for 81 per cent of unit sales (*see* Chapter 1). The latter half of the year saw the launch of the sub £1,000 Qume Crystalprint printing at 6 pages per minute, an area of the market that is now growing. In spite of this the best selling model in the category was the Epson GQ3500 (now superseded by the GQ5000) whilst Kyocera and the F1000 figured prominently in the 10 pages per minute section. In the 11 to 18 pages per minute category (accounting for nearly 3 per cent of the market by units), the Toshiba Pagelaser 12 and 11 pages per minute Panasonic KX-P4450 were close contenders with the Panasonic device just winning.

OFFICE LASERS

The printer that has been accorded the leading position for reasons of compactness, affordability, ease of use and offering the best emulations and upgrade options is the Hewlett-Packard LaserJet Series II. This accounts for about 45 per cent of all laser sales. Based on the superb Canon engine, the machine is also sold as the Series IID. List prices are £1,999 and £2,999 respectively while it's possible to obtain discounts to reach £1,400 and £2,100 respectively. Print speed is quoted at 8 pages per minute and a PostScript option is available for under £2,000. Maximum monthly volume is about 5,000 pages. Among the Series IID's attributes are twin paper bins and auto-duplex for double-sided printing.

Canon has created the world's best-selling laser engine. Despite this fact, the company cannot get top place with its own printer. Recently, the company offered HP emulation on its machine, but only on an extra disk. It is not a resident feature of the LBP-8II. Now, Canon has released the LBP-8III series which includes scalable fonts and vector graphics, and offers enhanced graphics ability combined with a faster processing speed for double performance. Major software companies such as Digital Research, MicroPro International, Lotus, Microsoft Corporation and the WordPerfect Corporation are supporting the LBP-8III's facilities by writing device drivers that enable their software to operate with the new range.

Canon has created the world's best-selling laser engine, but it cannot get top place with its own printer

The twin bin LBP-8IIIT and LBP-8IIIR duplex printer and basic LBP-8III model incorporate a controller which allows for internal font scaling and nine resident fonts comprising four

Dutch, four Swiss and Symbol. Fonts can be scaled in fractional increments from one point up to a maximum size that is dependent on memory. It supports character rotation, enlargement and reduction and special effects including user defined pattern fills, drop shadow, outline fonts and mirroring of the character grid. Also, 22 additional fonts are available on an optional plug-in card format. Memory is expandable up to 4.5 Megabytes. List prices are £2,745, £2,995 and £2,195 respectively. The interesting point is that Canon is not going to sell the new system to other companies so they can then sell it with their badges affixed.

Genicom has taken Canon's 400 dots per inch resolution OEM engine and incorporated two processors in its 6000 Series units, one for text and the other for graphics. The units have two page description languages: GeniScript which is PostScript compatible and ACE which is Genicom's own development. Printer emulations offered are HP's LaserJet Series II, IBM Graphics Printer and Diablo 630. Application drivers are Microsoft Windows, Digital Research GEM2 and GEM3 Applications, Microsoft Word, Ventura Publisher, Advent Desktop Publishing and Autocad. Recommended duty cycle is 5,000 pages per month, while the toner/drum cartridge has a 4,000 page life. The 6140 which comes with 1 Megabyte of memory costs £3,295 and is the office laser for wordprocessing applications. The 6142 which comes with 3 Megabytes of memory costs £3,795 and is the DTP laser.

Care should be taken about jumping straight into 400 dots per inch. Most existing software has been prepared for 300 dots per inch machines

However, care should be taken about jumping straight into 400 dots per inch. Remember that most existing software will

WHICH PRINTER FOR A PARTICULAR APPLICATION? 155

have been prepared for 300 dots per inch machines.

Other, good value Canon engine-based lasers are the Brother HL-8, Olivetti PG 208 M2 and Star Laserprinter 8.

On the surface, there's a lot going for the Brother HL-8. It offers more emulations than Hewlett-Packard's unit, and some extra fonts. But it has a maximum monthly volume of 3,000 pages, doesn't offer a PostScript option and is list priced at £2,195 (or, shopping around, for about £1,500). Unless you want all the offerings on the unit, it might pay to stay with the standard (and cheaper) HP and know you will be able to use the HP options of the JetScript board, soft fonts and font cartridges.

The Olivetti PG 208 M2 is a Hewlett-Packard LaserJet Series II lookalike, save for the control panel. The Olivetti printer behaves more like the HP device than any other Canon engine-based laser on the market. But then why pay £2,185 (list) or £1,500 (shopping around) when you can get the HP unit for less and be certain you've got all those HP and third party options on board as well.

List priced similarly to the foregoing units, the Star Laserprinter 8 offers more than the HP LaserJet in the way of fonts, emulations and memory. However, it is hard to guarantee that HP options such as the large font library will work on non-HP printers. The inevitable conclusion is that people wishing to play safe will choose Hewlett-Packard, even though they will get a little bit less laser printer for their outlay.

Citizen offers its Overture series of laser printers. The top-of-the-range 112 (list price £2395) runs at 12 pages per minute and emulates the HP Laserjet II as well as the Diablo 630. Emulations of the IBM Proprinter and Epson FX are optional. Both the 112, as well as the 110 10 pages per minute machine, have Mita engines. Citizen's 6 pages per minute Overture 106 (list price £1595), powered by a Sharp engine, is said to be one of the smallest units around.

The Kyocera F-1000 and F-1200 units feature engines made by Kyocera itself. Although not as widely known as HP and Canon, the Kyocera name brings worthy competition to HP in the form of good value for money. These are 10 pages per minute units which offer multiple emulations and fonts as standard (expensive options on most printers today). Print quality is not as highly rated as the Canon's and the machines make use of Kyocera's own page description language Prescribe and Advanced Prescribe. Special effects are possible using these, such as font rotation. Consumables come separately, and are cheaper than Canon's disposable cartridge system but are less convenient to use. They are nonetheless good value and the F-1200 is good for processing graphics with its 3.5 Megabytes of random access memory. List prices are £2,320 and £3,460 respectively, while discounts should make it possible to buy them for £1,750 and £2,550.

In 1990, IBM launched its 10 ppm 4019 laser printer for PCs, pricing it at £1926.

Panasonic manufactures and markets its KX-P4450 machine with a list price of £2,100 (it's possible to buy one for about £1,500). The obvious target is Hewlett-Packard and as with many other manufacturers Panasonic has squeezed in more for your money. Printing at 11 pages per minute, the unit has many emulations and is supplied with dual bin sheet feeder. An envelope tray is an option. There's a full on-site warranty for a year, or 60,000 pages if that comes first (*see* Chapter 7).

The Toshiba PageLaser 12 is intended for the 10,000 pages per month market and operates at 12 pages per minute. With an engine manufactured by Toshiba, the printer is more highly rated technically than the Panasonic (above) although the Panasonic pipped it in market share. The device features low consumables costs per page and is intended for high volume markets. The company is to market low cost A3 lasers (the PageLaser 8) and a PostScript version (the PageLaser 8PS) at list prices of £2,295 and £3,495 respectively.

Despite some problems with the GQ3500, Epson still managed to secure top place in the 6 pages per minute category with it in 1988, in part due to user favourable discounting. List price is £1,799, but it's possible to get one for about £1,100. However, the company is now selling the Ricoh engine-based GQ5000 which features a second generation print engine, the options of coax and twinax interfaces for connectivity to IBM mini and mainframe systems (*see* Chapter 3) and the GQ5000 maintenance programme.

Under this you're guaranteed to get an Epson approved engineer at your premises within eight working hours. Whether your GQ requires routine refurbishment or complex overhaul, you'll receive all warranty maintenance free of charge. A 250 sheet paper tray is another option for longer print runs, to augment the standard 150 sheet feeder.

Qume's CrystalPrint Series II is based on liquid crystal shutter (LCS) technology, which promises greater reliability plus lower costs than laser technology. List price for this unit is £1,495 while discounting will see the price reduced to about £1,100. It produces good print quality for a highly competitive price, which makes it attractive.

However, its paper tray only holds 100 sheets, it operates at 6 pages per minute and you'll need a service contract (no bad thing) as to replace the fuser (every 30,000 pages) requires an engineer. The text and graphics produced are indistinguishable from those of a laser. Included in the emulations offered is LaserJet Series II, which definitely adds to this printer's overall value.

POSTSCRIPT LASERS

The PostScript page description language (PDL) was incorporated by Apple into its Laserwriter in 1985 and since then the two products have become synonymous. PostScript offers excellent font and graphics flexibility and is practically indispensable for desktop publishing applications. In 1988 the Apple Laserwriter IINT and Laserwriter IINTX accounted for 70 per cent of PostScript sales. The rest comprised PostScript clones, PostScript upgrade cards and alternative PDLs.

Top place goes to the Apple Laserwriter IINTX. List price is £4,595 while shopping around should bring this to about £3,550. Based on the Canon SX engine and a Motorola 68020 processor, the unit offers a letter quality which is eminently suited for desktop publishing applications. Also featured is the HP LaserJet Plus emulation which comes in handy for software which doesn't support PostScript. In its most basic form, the printer is equipped with 2 Megabytes of random access memory. Its maximum capacity is 12 Megabytes which is reached in 1 Megabyte stages (at £250 a shot). The output is most commendable.

PostScript runs with user-friendly interface software to prepare the printed page. Behind the interface DTP software determines exactly where on the page the words and graphics should be placed

The current PostScript is offered by some larger PC manufacturers such as IBM and Apple as a standard PDL. Other companies such as Kyocera and Genicom have developed their own PostScript compatible PDL.

PostScript runs with user-friendly interface software to prepare the printed page. Behind the interface run DTP software packages which determine precisely at which point on the page the words and graphics should be placed. As PostScript is an interpretive language the statements are not turned into machine language until program execution. However, this activity does not take place in the system computer, but in a special computer which is built into the laser printer, which explains why PostScript capable laser printers are more expensive than standard lasers.

On the Kyocera F-series laser printers, the PDL Prescribe works in a similar way. However, the F-2200 and F-3000 are rather expensive - list prices are £4,760 and £6,600 respectively and discounted prices about £3,500 and £4,800. It is really up to the user to decide whether (assuming the necessary budget is available) to choose these undoubtedly feature-packed units, or opt for PostScript, which offers a guaranteed compatibility.

RECENT ANNOUNCEMENTS

Early in 1990, some new laser printers were announced.

The IBM LaserPrinter E uses a 5 pages per minute engine from Okidata. It outputs letter quality text and graphics at 300 x 300 dots per inch; data stream, graphics and paper-handling capabilities are identical to those of the IBM LaserPrinter, using the same single-element print cartridge, and supports the Printer Sharing Option and all the optional paper-handling features, memory cards, font cards, downloadable font packages and PostScript options on the IBM LaserPrinter. It has been selling in the USA at about

$1500. The machine can also be converted to the 10 pages per minute unit, available from June 1990 at about £2000. A PostScript interpreter is also offered with 17 scalable Adobe typeface programs; additionally, there is a version with an interpreter and an outline font card with another 22 scalable Adobe typefaces.

The recently-announced Okilaser 400 is a 4 pages per minute printer which uses LED imaging with dry monocomponent toner. It has 300 x 300 dots per inch resolution, HP Laserjet Series II emulation, 25 resident fonts, plug-in font cartridges, serial or parallel interfaces, with up to 2.5 Mbyte memory. There is one font card slot. This model is better than the Oki Laserline 6-Elite, a 6 pages per minute Ricoh engine-based machine, which is not as good as other Canon-based units in terms of print quality and maintenance. It has a list price of £1249 for a basic unit, but shopping around it should be possible to buy one for around £1000.

The Okilaser 800 is an 8 pages per minute printer, using the same print technology as the 400 model. It has single and dual bin versions, 3 resident emulations, 35 resident fonts, twin plug-in font cartridges, resident serial/parallel interfaces, dual port interface options, with up to 4.5 Mbyte memory. The single-bin model has a list price of £1799; the dual-bin retails at £1999. By shopping around, it should be possible to buy these machines for around £1500 and £1700 respectively.

INK JET PRINTERS

Hewlett-Packard's launch of its Deskjet recently gave the inkjet market a tremendous boost. In the past two years it was the inkjet market which showed the greatest unit and value growth of 128 per cent and 135 per cent respectively. This resulted in inkjet printers accounting for a 5 per cent share of

WHICH PRINTER FOR A PARTICULAR APPLICATION?

the total printer market in number of units sold. This is expected to grow significantly in the years ahead.

Pride of place goes undoubtedly to the HP Deskjet which is listed at just under £800, but can be bought at discount for £575 or so. HP made a massive success in the laser market by taking a Canon machine, adding a Printer Command Language and performing marketing marvels - it's now the dominant laser printer standard. Watch now for a repeat with ink jet technology, for HP has again taken Canon machines. The two do offer different emulations and case designs though.

Unless you bought a daisywheel, no printer costing this little comes close to offering the print quality. Its draft output is also better than the quality you can get from a matrix printer. Print speed is 240 characters per second at 10 characters per inch in draft quality mode or 120 characters per second in NLQ mode. The disadvantages include higher consumables costs than for a laser - so don't buy it instead of the laser if you've got a high volume workload. To make use of letter quality print, additional fonts are **de rigueur**, but soft fonts require extra buffer memory (buffer size on the unit is 16k).

The disadvantages of inkjet printers include higher consumable costs than for lasers - so don't buy one instead of a laser unless you've got a high volume workload

The Deskjet is an excellent buy as a low cost letter quality printer for low volume applications. As with all HP printers, the warranty is 12 months on-site. The Canon BJ-130 is again a superb machine with a similar pricing structure to HP's. Emulations are IBM Proprinter as standard and NEC P7 optional (against HP's PCL Level 3 as standard and Epson FX-80 optional).

Canon offer a sheet feeder as standard and buffer size of 32k. Again it's very good for low cost letter quality printing. In situations where absolute quiet is a must and a laser printer is too expensive or oversized paper is needed, the Canon BJ-130 is definitively a good buy.

Dataproducts' SI 480 uses solid ink pellets which are melted on to the page to produce one of the best letter quality printers around. List pricing is £2,195 while you should be able to buy one for about £1,650. This printer will appeal to you if you need the ultimate in letter quality but do not need a laser's text and graphics flexibility. It's not as versatile as a laser and much too well specified to double up as a matrix. Its emulations are Dataproducts 8070, IBM Colour jet, IBM Graphics, IBM Proprinter and IBM Quietwriter II, ie it doesn't have a modern emulation.

However, many software programs are expected to provide printer drivers in the near future. Its speed of operation is similar to the HP and Canon units, while its noise level in operation is practically zero.

Epson's SQ-2550 supersedes the SQ-2500 which was much more expensive than the printers already mentioned (list price £1,349) and for that reason could be obtained for, at the most, £900. The launches of the HP DeskJet and Canon BJ-130 were not good news for this printer, which actually was the top-selling model by value.

The SQ-2550 redresses any imperfections in print quality of its predecessor, and offers draft printing speeds of 600 characters per second (at 10 characters per inch). Letter quality is throughput at up to 190 characters per second. Graphics capability is offered at 360 dots per inch resolution while options are a pull-feed tractor, single and double bin cut sheet feeders and the twinax and coax interfaces for connectivity with IBM mini and mainframe systems, plus the IEEE-488 interface. Ink is loaded using fully-sealed cartridges. Epson's warranty on maintenance is also, like HP's, free and on-site.

Mannesmann Tally is aiming its MT91 printer (list price £795) at the high quality output, low noise and low price tag market (eg applications such as high quality wordprocessing and spreadsheets where a large carriage width is critical, since the MT91 prints on to paper up to A3 size). The unit can print on to plain paper from 52 to 81 g per square metre, and offers dual print speeds of 220 characters per second (high speed) and 110 characters per second (high quality).

The resolution is 360 dots per inch, while IBM Proprinter emulation is standard. Depending on which print mode is chosen, print head life is 100 up to 200 million characters. Options available include NEC P7 emulation, slots for additional font cartridges, RS-232 serial interface (Centronics parallel is standard) and a pin feed tractor device. By Spring 1990, Mannesmann Tally wants 10 per cent of the UK ink jet market.

The Diconix 300 and 300W, available through the Kodak Personal Printer Products Group in the UK, retail for £499 and £599 respectively. Fed by ink cartridges (500,000 characters or 500 pages - compared with several million characters for most dot matrix ribbons), the Diconix units are 12 nozzle machines which are considered good for office workers who have infrequent printing needs and laptop users who need a portable printer.

The disadvantages are print quality (ie, not as good as the above mentioned devices) and the need to change cartridges frequently. But if you're after quietness and a small size of printer (eg, you can slide one on to a shelf in your crowded office or into a briefcase with ease), these could be for you.

Howtek's Pixelmaster is a floor-standing colour printer which uses a revolutionary hot ink jet technology called Thermo Jet to produce high quality images and fine text. Its price, at £4,135 for a basic machine tends to put it in a different league. Applications are in preview printing for Computer Aided Design/Computer Aided Manufacturing (CAD/CAM) and for presentation quality graphics. With quoted speeds of 20 seconds for a mono page and 3.2 minutes for a full colour image (up to 250,000 different shades are achievable by mixing cyan, magenta, yellow and black), the printer uses ink pellets and prints on to ordinary paper and acetates.

Resolution is 240 x 240 dots per inch. The printing process involves the paper being fed past the rotating print head, whereupon a piezo electric crystal system fires the hot plastic ink onto the page. The ink solidifies as soon as it hits the paper, with the result that the image has a professional embossed effect.

THERMAL TRANSFER PRINTERS

According to market research company Romtec, thermal transfer printers achieved a 5 per cent unit and 6 per cent value share in 1988. However, by 1993 the unit share obtained by thermal printers is expected to show an average annual growth of 12 per cent and account for 6 per cent of total sales, whilst a slightly reduced value share of 5 per cent reflects an average annual growth rate of 14 per cent. Thermal transfer, along with laser, LED, LCS and ink jet technologies, constitutes the vanguard that's going to usurp the hitherto long enjoyed supremacy of dot matrix impact technology.

The thermal transfer market is dominated by IBM with its

QuietWriter III. With a list price of £1,096 and the possibility of getting one for about £800, the 5202 QuietWriter III printer produces solid letter quality which is better than that from a laser, although it's not so good on resolution.

Draft speeds at 10 characters per inch are 270 characters per second, while letter quality speeds are 100 characters per second. Up to now, the running costs have been nearly prohibitive at about 10p per page.

Emulations are IBM QuietWriter and IBM Proprinter, while there is a parallel interface included in the price. As well as producing very good text quality, this unit can print graphics and a wide selection of fonts (resident fonts are Courier and Boldface PS, while downloadable fonts are optional at £132, which includes a download cartridge for storing fonts). Cut sheet feeders (single bin, dual bin and envelope tray) which are options on the QuietWriter III also fit the 5204 QuickWriter. If all you are printing out are letters, though, you could be better off looking at the QuickWriter, which although looking more expensive initially will be cheaper on consumables.

Olivetti market a cross-licensed version of IBM's QuietWriter II, known as the TH 760 S. Text quality is superb, but again there are high costs of consumables in running the unit which work out at anything up to 11p per page. You'll also at some time need a print head cleaning cartridge, which will add to the running costs. If you are really intent on getting into thermal transfer at this level, the IBM QuietWriter III is faster and by definition better. The emulations the Olivetti unit offers are Epson FX-80, IBM Proprinter and IBM Quietwriter II. A parallel interface is included in the price (list £859, but with discount about £640).

Oki's Okimate 20 is a well-established thermal transfer

printer at the low end of the printing spectrum. Thermal transfer lends itself to colour printing and the Mitsubishi G650 thermal transfer colour engine is being used in the first full colour PostScript printer, the QMS ColorScript 100, which costs less than £20,000, prints at a resolution of 300 dots per inch and handles paper sizes up to A3. The Mitsubishi G330, which costs under £3,000, avoids the problem of software drivers by taking images on the computer's display screen and converting them to print commands.

Much activity is also underway in company development laboratories. Epson, for example, has a thermal transfer printer, as will most if not all other Japanese companies - plus other non-Far Eastern concerns who will want to badge products as their own. It will be worthwhile to monitor the technical press over the coming years to discover what emanates from these laboratories.

LINE PRINTERS

In the six years leading to 1992, market research companies IDC and Dataquest expect the market share of impact line printers in Europe to decrease by 6.1 per cent per year, in terms of sales growth. Almost exclusively, market share will be lost to the phenomenal rise of the page printer, due to the increasing acceptance and popularity of laser printers in business, especially in the field of desktop publishing and networking.

This is most definitely not to say that line printers are being squeezed out of existence. They are holding their own in terms of numbers of installations and sales (*see* Chapter 1).

Within this category, about which any user will be fully conversant, are shuttle matrix printers, band printers, ion deposition printers, magnetographic printers and high end laser printers.

It is not the intention of this book to state, for example, that all IBM or ICL systems should run with Dataproducts or Genicom or Toadflax band printers, because this is an area of more complexity than an office environment. The Management Information Services personnel populating the computer centres, data processing departments or whatever, know the set ups and workloads of their configurations inside out. However, this book would come in useful in such locations where the outermost parts of the corporate are setting up networks, installing stand-alone micros or wanting to initiate a micro to mainframe link.

The people at the end of these tentacles do need information about suitable printers - becoming more computer literate would then enable them to appreciate the workings of the MIS function.

APPENDIX 1

QUICK PRICE GUIDE

This guide gives an indication only of the discounted prices you can expect to find for defined classes of printer - refer also to the notes on pricing contained in Chapter 9.

UNDER £250
Mainly 9-pin matrix printers, although it is possible to get the Qume LetterPro for about £245.

UNDER £350
Again, mainly 9-pin matrix printers. Also the Brother HR-20 daisywheel, Hewlett-Packard ThinkJet inkjet and a clutch of 24-pin matrix printers (eg, Epson LQ-500, Star LC24-10 and NEC Pinwriter P2200).

UNDER £400
Once more, there are many 9-pin matrix printers (eg, Oki Microline 320, Mannesmann Tally MT86, Citizen MSP-45 and 50). The Hewlett-Packard QuietJet inkjet and Citizen HQP-40 and Swift-64 24-pin dot matrix printer.

UNDER £450
Star and Panasonic feature with 24-pin matrix devices, and there's the Hewlett-Packard QuietJet+ inkjet and Oki Microline 292 Elite 18-pin matrix printers. Otherwise, 9-pin machines, eg Epson FX range, Olivetti, Fujitsu, IBM Proprinter, Seikosha and Panasonic.

UNDER £550
A sprinkling of 9-pin matrix printers from Star, Citizen, Fujitsu, Oki and Epson, while 24-pin devices start to appear, eg Epson, IBM, NEC, Citizen, Olivetti, Fujitsu, Toshiba, Mannesmann Tally.

UNDER £700
Canon's BJ-130 and Hewlett-Packard's DeskJet ink jet devices, Olivetti's TH 760 S thermal transfer printer,

QUICK PRICE GUIDE 171

Mannesmann Tally MT290 9-pin matrix printer, two 18-pin devices (from Oki and MT) and a clutch of 24-pin units are in this band. Epson's LQ-1050, IBM Proprinter XL24 and NEC Pinwriter P7 Plus all feature, as does the Fujitsu DL3400 and Star NB-15.

UNDER £1,000
Two daisywheels (Olivetti and Brother) and a combined daisywheel/matrix unit, IBM's Quietwriter III thermal transfer and Epson's SQ inkjet all feature here. Plus the Qume liquid crystal CrystalPrint. The rest is pure 24-pin matrix, eg Epson LQ-2550, IBM Quickwriter, Fujitsu DL2600.

UNDER £1,500
True laser printers appear, eg Hewlett-Packard, Epson, Citizen, IBM and Oki, a Fujitsu LED unit, and Qume CrystalPrint. Also upmarket 24-pin matrix machines from Fujitsu and Brother, 18-pins from Brother and Olivetti, and the rugged 9-pin matrix from Epson, the DFX-5000.

UNDER £2,500
With the exception of Seikosha's 18-pin matrix machine and Dataproducts inkjet unit, this is the realm of the laser and an LED unit from NEC.

OVER £2,500
Pure laser and LED (NEC and IBM). Names include Apple, Dataproducts, IBM, Mannesmann Tally, Kyocera, Fujitsu and Qume.

UNDER £5,000
A sort of grey area approaching the shuttle matrix and band printer camps, which is another area of computing entirely. As a rule, 400 lines per minute band printers have a list price about £4,900 while 400 lines per minute shuttle matrix printers are listed at about £5,240.

UNDER £7,000
The domain of 800 lines per minute shuttle matrix and band printers

UNDER £9,000
Here are to be found 1,000 lines per minute shuttle matrix and band printers

UNDER £11-£12,000
Shuttle matrix and band printers in the speed ranges 1,200 to 1,400 lines per minute

ABOVE £12,000
The higher up the price range one goes, the more complex both the technology and the printers themselves become. At this level of cost, you are dealing with massive throughputs and high volume of data to be output.

APPENDIX 2

MANUFACTURERS' NAMES AND ADDRESSES

WHERE TO GET A PRINTER
List of Manufacturers and/or Subsidiaries

AMSTRAD plc
Brentwood House, 169 King's Road, Brentwood, Essex.
Tel: 0277 228888
9, 18 and 24-pin matrix printers

AMT
General Audio & Data, 91/92 Akeman Street, Tring, Hertfordshire HP23 6AJ.
Tel: (044282) 8681
24-pin matrix printers

APPLE COMPUTER (UK) Ltd
Eastman Way, Hemel Hempstead, Hertfordshire.
Tel: 0442 60244
Laser printers - the standard bearer for PostScript laser printers

BROTHER OFFICE EQUIPMENT DIVISION
Shepley Street, Audenshaw, Manchester M34 5JD.
Tel: 061 330 6531
Laser printers; daisywheel printers; 9, 18 and 24-pin matrix printers

BULL
Honeywell House, Great West Road, Brentford, Middlesex TW8 9DH.
Tel: 081 568 9191
Matrix printers; band printers; laser printers

CANON UK Ltd
Canon House, Manor Road, Wallington, Surrey.
Tel: 081 773 3173

MANUFACTURERS' NAMES AND ADDRESSES 175

Laser printers (the company is *the* laser printer hardware manufacturer and its laser engine is the driving force behind many of those on the market. Also, Canon manufactures all the supplies used by all Canon engine lasers worldwide); bubble inkjet printers

CITIZEN EUROPE Ltd
Wellington House, 4/10 Cowley Road, Uxbridge, Middlesex UB8 2XW.
Tel: 0895 72621
Laser printers; 9 and 24-pin matrix printers

COMPAREX INFORMATION SYSTEMS
BASF House, 151 Wembley Park Drive, Wembley, Middlesex HA9 8JG.
Tel: 081 908 3100
Band printers; high end laser printers

COMPASS PERIPHERAL SYSTEMS
Unity House, Kennet Side, Newbury, Berkshire RG14 5PX.
Tel: (0635) 521600
Band printers; laser printers; 9 and 24-pin matrix printers

COMPUPRINT
The printers' division of Bull HN Information Systems Italia
Maxted Road, Hemel Hempstead, Hertfordshire HP2 7DZ.
Tel: (0442) 232222
9 and 18-pin matrix printers; laser printers

DATAPRODUCTS Ltd
Dataproducts House, Unit 1, Heron Industrial Estate, Spencers Wood, Reading, Berkshire RG7 1PG.
Tel: (0734) 884777
Laser printers; solid ink printers; pin matrix printers; shuttle matrix printers; band printers

DECISION DATA COMPUTER (GB) Ltd
Decision Data House, 91-93 Windmill Road, Sunbury on Thames, Middlesex TW16 7EF.
Tel: (0932) 788788
Shuttle matrix printers; band printers

DICONIX
The Kodak Personal Printer Products Group, Kodak Copy Products Division, Kodak House, Station Road, Hemel Hempstead, Hertfordshire HP1 1JU.
Tel: (0442) 61122
Inkjet printers

DIGITAL EQUIPMENT CO
Digital Park, Imperial Way, Reading, Berkshire RG2 0TE.
Tel: (0734) 868711
Shuttle matrix printers; band printers; pin matrix printers

EPSON (UK) Ltd
Campus 100, Maylands Avenue, Hemel Hempstead, Herts HP2 7EZ.
Tel: 0442 61144
Laser printers; 9, 24 and 48 pin matrix printers (the company has the *de facto* standard worldwide for matrix printers - all matrix printers marketed today invariably offer Epson FX emulation for 9-pin and Epson LQ emulation for 24-pin, if they want to be competitive); ink jet printers; thermal transfer printers

ERSKINE PRINTING SYSTEMS LTD
Katana House, Fort Fareham, Fareham, Hampshire PO14 1AH.
Tel: (0329) 221121
Laser printers

FACIT
Maidstone Road, Rochester, Kent ME1 3QN.
Tel: (0634) 830008
9, 18 and 24-pin matrix printers; daisywheel printers

FUJITSU EUROPE Ltd
2 Longwalk Road, Stockley Park, Uxbridge, Middlesex.
Tel: 081 573 4444
Laser printers, including a LED printer; 24-pin matrix printers; band printers

GENICOM Ltd
Armstrong Mall, Southwood, Farnborough, Hampshire GU14 0NR.
Tel: (0252) 522500
Shuttle matrix printers; band printers; 9, 18 and 24-pin matrix printers Incorporates the Centronics range of printers

GESTETNER DATA SYSTEMS Ltd
210 Euston Road, London NW1 2DA.
Tel: 071 387 7021
Laser printers

HARRIS SYSTEMS Ltd
Eskdale Road, Winnersh, Wokingham, Berkshire RG11 5TR.
Tel: (0734) 698787
Shuttle matrix printers; band printers

HERMES PRECISA
Hermes House, Ipswich Road, Colchester, Essex CO4 4EG.
Tel: (0206) 845251
Thermal transfer printers; laser printers; dot matrix printers

HEWLETT-PACKARD Ltd
Miller House, The Ring, Bracknell, Berkshire RG12 1XN.
Tel: (0344) 424898
Laser printers (the company has set the standard for laser printers); inkjet technology (again it's a leader); shuttle matrix printers; 24-pin matrix printers

HOWTEK
see Techex
Pixelmaster colour printer

IBM UNITED KINGDOM Ltd
National Enquiry Centre, 389 Chiswick High Road, London W4 4AL.
Tel: 081 747 0747
Thermal transfer printers; laser or page printers one with LED engine; mainframe laser printers; 9 and 24-pin matrix printers; various line printers

ICL
Bridge House, Putney Bridge, Fulham, London SW6 3JX.
Tel: 081-788 7272
Band printers; mainframe laser printers; pin matrix printers

INFORMATION TECHNOLOGY Ltd
Maylands Avenue, Hemel Hempstead, Hertfordshire HP2 7DF.
Tel: (0442) 42277
Band printers; pin matrix printers

INTEGREX Ltd
Church Gresley, Burton-on-Trent, Staffordshire DE11 9PT.
Tel: (0283) 215432
Inkjet printers

C.ITOH ELECTRONICS CO Ltd
Beacon House, 26/28 Worple Road, Wimbledon, London SW19 4EE.
Tel: 081 946 4690
Shuttle matrix printers; laser printers; 24-pin matrix printers; ion deposition printers

KYOCERA ELECTRONICS
8 Beacontree Plaza, Gillette Way, Reading, Berkshire RG2 0BP.
Tel: (0734) 311500
Laser printers

MANNESMANN TALLY Ltd
Molly Millars Lane, Wokingham, Berkshire RG11 2QT.
Tel: (0734) 788711
Shuttle matrix printers; various line printers; 9 and 24-pin matrix printers; laser printers; inkjet and bubble inkjet printers

MEMOREX TELEX Ltd
96 - 104 Church Street, Staines, Middlesex TW18 4XU.
Tel: (0784) 51488
Shuttle matrix printers; magnetographic printers

MITSUBISHI ELECTRIC UK Ltd
Electronics Division, Travellers Lane, Hatfield, Herts AL10 8XB.
Tel: (07072) 76100
Thermal transfer printers

NCR Ltd
206 Marylebone Road, London NW1 6LY.
Tel: 071 723 7070
Band printers; pin matrix printers

NEC BUSINESS SYSTEMS (EUROPE) Ltd
NEC House, 1 Victoria Road, London W3 6BR.
Tel: 081 993 8111
Laser - really LED - printers; 24-pin matrix printers (highly regarded)

NEWBURY DATA RECORDING
Hawthorne Road, Staines, Middlesex TW18 3BJ.
Tel: (0784) 461500
Matrix printers; laser printers; line printers

NIXDORF COMPUTER
Nixdorf House, Oldbury, Bracknell, Berkshire RG12 4FZ.
Tel: (0344) 862222
Band printers; matrix printers

OKI
Technitron Data Ltd, 750/751 Deal Avenue, Slough Trading Estate, Slough, Berkshire SL1 4SH.
Tel: (0753) 31292
Laser printers; 9, 18 and 24-pin matrix printers

OLIVETTI
British Olivetti Ltd, 86/88 Upper Richmond Road, London SW15 2UR.
Tel: 081 789 6699
Laser printers; thermal transfer printers; daisywheel printers; 9, 18 and 24-pin matrix printers

OLYMPIA
Intelligent Interfaces, 43B Wood Street, Stratford-upon-Avon, Warwickshire CV37 6JQ.
Tel: (0789) 415875
9-pin matrix printers

PANASONIC INDUSTRIAL UK Ltd
280-290 Bath Road, Slough, Berkshire SL1 6JG.
Tel: (0753) 73181
Laser printers; 9 and 24-pin matrix printers

PHILIPS BUSINESS SYSTEMS
Elektra House, 2 Bergholt Road, Colchester CO4 5BE.
Tel: (0206) 575115
Matrix printers

PRIME COMPUTER (UK) Ltd
Primos House, 2-4 Lampton Road, Hounslow, Middlesex TW3 1 JW.
Tel: 081 572 7400
Band printers; shuttle matrix printers

PRINTRONIX Ltd
Loddon Vale House, Suite B, Hurricane Way, Woodley, Berkshire RG5 4UX.
Tel: (0734) 441055
Shuttle matrix printers

QMS EUROPE BV
Utrecht, The Netherlands.
Tel: 010 31 30 420129
Laser printers; colour PostScript printers; thermal transfer printers

QUME UK Ltd
Qume House, Park Way, Newbury, Berkshire RG13 1EE.
Tel: (0635) 523200
Laser printers, including liquid crystal shutter printers; daisywheel printers

RANK XEROX
Parkway, Marlow, Buckinghamshire SL7 1YL.
Tel: (0628) 890000
Mainframe printing at 5,000 lines per minute plus

RBS SYSTEMS LTD
141/5 Curtain Road, London EC2A 3QE.
Tel: 071 739 4106
Laser printers; solid ink printers

SEIKOSHA (UK) Ltd Unit 14, Newlands Drive, Colnbrook, Slough, Berkshire SL3 0DX.
Tel: (0753) 685873
9, 18 and 24-pin matrix printers; LED printers

SET UK Ltd
Axis 5, Rhodes Way, Watford, Hertfordshire WD2 4YW.
Tel: (0923) 32055
High end laser printers (42 and 215 pages per minute)

SIEMENS
Data Systems Division, St Catherines House, 2 Hanworth Road, Feltham, Middlesex TW13 5DF.
Tel: (0932) 785691
High end laser printers; inkjet printers

STAR MICRONICS UK Ltd
Craven House, 40 Uxbridge Road, Ealing, London W5 2BS.
Tel: 081 840 1800
Laser printers; 9 and 24-pin matrix printers

STORAGE TECHNOLOGY
Storagetek House, Woking Business Park, Albert Drive, Woking, Surrey GU21 5JY.
Tel: (04862) 27331
Band printers; high end laser printers

TANDY
InterTan, Tandy Centre, Leamore Lane, Bloxwich, West Midlands WS2 7PS.
Tel: (0922) 710000
24-pin matrix printers

TAXAN
Taxan House, Cookham Road, Bracknell, Berkshire RG12 1RB.
Tel: (0344) 484646
Dot matrix printers

TECHEX Ltd
Meridien House, 100 Hanger Lane, London W5 1EZ.
Tel: 081 991 0121
Howtek Pixelmaster 'hot' inkjet printer supplier

TEKTRONIX (UK) LTD
Fourth Avenue, Globe Park, Marlow, Buckinghamshire SL7 1YD.
Tel: (04284) 6000
Colour PostScript printer which also accepts HPGL (Hewlett-Packard's plotter command language)

TOSHIBA INFORMATION SYSTEMS LTD
Toshiba Court, Weybridge Business Park, Addlestone Road, Weybridge, Surrey KT15 2UL.
Tel: (0932) 841600
Thermal printers; laser printers (the company was the first to produce an A3 laser); dot matrix printers

WENGER PRINTERS LTD
Unit 10, The Valley Centre, Gordon Road, High Wycombe, Buckinghamshire HP13 6EQ.
Tel: (0494) 450941
LCS printers; dot matrix printers

GLOSSARY

COMMONLY-USED PRINTER JARGON

ACE - a page description language with typesetting roots which is used on the Genicom 6000 Series desktop laser printers

AppleTalk - an interface which is used to link Apple computers with printers

ASCII - American Standard Code for Information Interchange. Standard computer codes used for the most common alphanumeric characters.

Baud rate - speed of communication between the computer and the printer in bits per second, which is only needed with serial interfaces.

Buffer - printer memory which permits the downloading of information prior to printing

CCD - charge coupled device

CE - Customer Engineer (IBM)

Centronics interface - standard parallel interface which is used to link computers with printers

Character set - complete list of all the characters that can be printed by a printer - also known as a symbol set

Coax - system of interfacing to IBM mainframe computers

CPI - characters per inch (*see also* Pitch)

CPS - characters per second, one measure of a printer's speed; others are lines per minute (LPM), pages per minute (PPM) and pages per hour (PPH)

Computer Aided Publishing - *see* DTP

GLOSSARY OF COMMONLY-USED PRINTER JARGON

Corporate electronic publishing - *see* DTP

CPI - characters per inch

CPS - characters per second

Daisywheel - impact printing method which uses preformed letters on separate stems of a plastic wheel

Developer - consumable item which is used to transfer toner to the drum in a laser printer

Diablo 630 - trademark of Xerox Corp; Diablo was a successful manufacturer of daisywheel printers whose products set the standard

DIN - German standards body

Drum - a light sensitive cylinder which is used in laser printers; an image of the page is produced on the drum by the laser whereupon toner sticks to it, being subsequently set onto sheets of paper to produce the print out

DTP - desktop publishing

Electronic publishing - *see* DTP

Emulation - the situation where a printer imitates another printer's response to the print commands transmitted by software packages

Engine - heart of the laser printer; the working bit that suppliers add to with fonts, emulations, interfaces and random access memory

EP cartridge - disposable electrophotographic cartridge used in laser printers based on the Canon engine, containing all consumables

EPPT - European Printer Performance Tests; a set of tests which is an attempt to measure the throughput of a printer rather than any measure of speed (*see* Chapter 2); promoted by nine European printer manufacturers

Epson EX, EX-800, FX-80, FX-80+, FX-85, FX-100, FX-105, FX-286, FX-800, LQ-800, LQ-1000, LQ-1500, LQ-2500, LX-800 - standard emulations for different types of printers, reflecting Epson's leading role in the printer field

ESC escape sequence - Epson Standard Code for printers, which is a series of standard printer commands

Fanfold - continuous stationery used with tractor feeders

Font - a group of characters in a specific size and style

Friction feed - a platen which guides single sheets of paper through a printer

Fuser - in a laser printer, this is the heat and pressure roller used to bond the toner to the paper

GeniScript - PostScript compatible page description language used on the Genicom 6000 series desktop laser printers

gsm - grams per square metre

HPGL - for plotter emulation, this is the Hewlett-Packard Graphics Language

HP LaserJet Plus - standard emulation for a laser printer

IBM Graphics Printer - standard emulation for a printer

IBM Proprinter XL, XL24 - standard emulations for a matrix printer

IBM Quietwriter III - standard emulation for a printer

IC cards/cartridges - integrated circuits held on plug-in cards or cartridges which hold extra fonts for printers or random access memory

IEEE - Institute of Electrical and Electronics Engineers (US)

Impact - printer technologies where wires or fully formed characters strike the page through a ribbon to produce the printed image; capable of being used to produce multi-part forms Ink jet - a printing technology in which characters are formed by firing dots of ink from a series of specially designed nozzles

Interface - a printer is linked to a computer via a cable at each end of which are special connectors called interfaces

I/O - input/output (of data) to and from a computer and/or its peripherals

Ion deposition - non-impact technology of printing; an ionic cartridge extends over the whole width of the aluminium oxide print drum, digital data sent to the ionic cartridge controls the shooting of ions onto the rotating surface of the print drum

ISO - International Standards Organisation

kB - kilobyte

Laser - light amplification by stimulated emission of radiation

LCS - *see* Liquid Crystal Shutter

LED - *see* Light Emitting Diode

Liquid Crystal Shutter (LCS) - a technology which is used as an alternative to the laser beam in page (ie, laser) printers

Light Emitting Diode (LED) - a technology which is used as an alternative to the laser beam in page (ie, laser) printers

LPM - lines per minute (*see also* CPS)

LQ - Letter Quality; output from a printer which is considered exceptionally good and suitable for preparing correspondence

Magnetographic - non-impact technology of printing which involves writing the page to be printed magnetically to a rotating drum, toning with magnetic ink, transferring the image to paper and fixing with heat

MB - megabyte

MTBF - mean time before failure

MTBSC - mean time between service calls

MTTF - mean time to failure

MTTR - mean time to repair

NLQ - Near Letter Quality; output from a printer which is considered good enough to be used for official letters; many printers work in draft and NLQ modes

Non-impact - printer technologies where the final image is produced without striking the page; consequently, these technologies are not suitable for producing multi-part forms

GLOSSARY OF COMMONLY-USED PRINTER JARGON

Off-line - a state in which the printer is still physically linked to the computer but where the printer will not print information it receives

Oki ML - standard printer emulation devolving from the Oki Microline range of printers

On-line - a state in which the printer will print any data it receives

OPC - organic photoconductor

Page printers - printers which print a page at a time, compared with serial printers (character at a time) and line printers (line at a time)

Paper parking - a system of paper management whereby there is no need to change feeders as it's all under push button command; when feeding single sheets, continuous paper is automatically reversed and held in place; when feeding continuous paper, single sheets are held ready in the cut sheet feeder (eg, on Epson LQ-1050 and LQ-850)

Parallel interface - an interface over which data is transmitted eight bits at a time

PC - personal computer

PCB - printed circuit board

PEP - Printer Enhancement Pack

Pitch - the number of characters a printer will print per inch, eg 10 pitch is normally written as 10 cpi (characters per inch), 12 pitch as 12 cpi, etc

pixel - picture point size

Point size - how the size of a character is measured

PostScript - Page Description Language developed by the company Adobe Systems which controls the output to certain printers, eg to laser or page printers in desktop publishing applications

PPH - pages per hour (*see also* CPS)

PPM - pages per minute (*see also* CPS)

Printer Command Language (PCL) - standard emulations used by Hewlett-Packard's printers

Printer driver - that part of a software program which controls the commands sent to the printer

Proportional spacing - where the space between successive characters is calculated in proportion to the width of each character, eg between characters such as w, m, l, i and t

Random Access Memory (RAM) - a type of memory from which data is lost when the power supply to the printer is turned off

RETAIN - Remote Technical Assistance and Information Network (IBM)

RS232 interface - a common type of serial interface

RSA - Retainer Service Agreement (IBM)

Serial interface - an interface over which data is transmitted one bit at a time

Serial printers - these are printers which print each character successively

Sheet feeders - these are containers which clip onto printers and are used to load, say, up to 250 cut sheets of paper into the printer automatically

Soft fonts - these are digital fonts stored on floppy disks which can be passed into a printer's memory

Thermal transfer - a printer technology whereby ink held on special ribbons is impressed on the paper by being heated through a matrix of electrodes

Thoric lens - single light points are focussed through this lens directly onto the electrostatically charged exposure drum in a laser printer

Toner - a powdered ink used in laser printers

Tractor feed - a mechanism for pulling continuous stationery through a printer

Transfer corona/scorotoron wire - a fine steel wire in a laser printer for the electrical charging of the exposure drum, and transmission wire for the generation of the electrical charge required for the toner transfer

Twinax - system of interfacing to IBM System/3X and AS/400 mid-range computer systems

WYSIWYG - What You See Is What You Get

INDEX

130 column fan-folded paper, 8
18-pin dot matrix printers, 7, 126, 144-145
  low cost, 130, 142
  medium price, 129, 144
  upmarket, 127-128, 144-145
1992, 30, 37
24-pin dot matrix printers, 3, 7, 50, 57, 104, 126, 145-151
  low price, 129, 146-147
  medium price, 128, 147-148
  upmarket, 127, 149-151
240 dots per inch, 27
370 series, 42
400 dots per inch, 27
48-pin matrix printers, 4
600 lines per minute, 9
9-pin dot matrix printers, 6, 50, 126, 140-142
  low price, 130, 142
  mid-price, 129, 142-143
  upmarket, 127-128, 143

A3 lasers, 157
A3 paper, 102, 135, 145, 163
A3 printing, 13, 18
accessories, 97-106
  costs of, 26
accounts work, 141
ACE page description language, 13, 154
acoustic hoods, 105
Adobe typeface programs, 73, 160
Advanced Prescribe, 156
Aldus, 70
Alternative Graphics Mode, 148
Alto Workstation, 70
Amstrad, 130, 174
AMT, 174
ANSI/ISO DP9636 standard, 139
Apple Computer (UK) Ltd, 174
  computers, 32, 49, 70, 73, 74, 124, 125
  Laserwriter, 158
AppleTalk, 31
application duty cycle, 33
Apricot, 124
ASCII characters, 59
ASCII files, 109
Ashton-Tate, 51, 52
Avant Garde (typeface), 76

backup, 117
band printers, 7, 8-9, 33, 133-134, 136, 171
  accesssories, 105-106
banking environment, printers in, 108-109
banks, 135
barcoding, 6, 134, 136
BASIC language, 74
baud rates, 48
bin feeders, 86
binary digits (bits), 45-46
bit map display, 73
bits (binary digits), 45

Bitstream, 53
Bodoni (typeface), 76
Bookman (typeface), 76
Brother, 124, 125, 130, 174
  18-pin matrix printers, 171
  24-pin matrix printers, 171
  daisywheel, 171
  HL-8, 155
  HR-20, 170
  HR-40, 130
  M-1209, 142
  M-2518, 129, 144
  M-4018, 128, 145
'bubble jet' printer, 132
buffer interface, 47
building societies, 135
built-in parallel interface, 31
bulk printing, 133
Bull, 29, 34, 110, 174
business forms, 19
bytes, 45-46

C.Itoh Electronics Ltd, 179
cable(s), 98
CAD, see Computer Aided Design
CAM, see Computer Aided Manufacturing
Canon, 10, 12, 50, 91, 103, 124, 131, 152, 174
  BJ-130, 132, 152, 161, 170
  laser engine, 29, 153, 158
  LBP-8 Mark III laser, 124
  LBP-8II, 153
Canon SX engine, 124
carbon ribbon, 127
carriage, wide, 129
cartridges, 52
Casio, 126
cassette, like used in office typewriter, 16
CCD, see charge coupled device
Centronics, 31
CEs, see Customer Engineers (IBM)
CGI, see computer-graphics interface
character density, 23
character set, 77
  international, 62
characters per inch (CPI), 34
characters per second (CPS), ratings, 33, 34
charge coupled device (CCD), 79
Citizen, 117, 125
  24-pin matrix printer, 170
  9-pin matrix printer, 170
  Europe, 175
  HQP-40, 170
  laser, 171
  MSP-45, 170
  MSP-50, 170
  Overture printers, 106, 155, 156
  ProDot 9/9x series, 24, 128, 129, 143, 148C

Swift-24, 129
Swift-64, 147
cleaning the printer, 54-55
coax/twinax, 42, 43, 44
code, production of, 5
colour printing, 6, 14, 16-17, 19, 102, 103, 104-105, 126, 133, 145, 148, 150
coloured thermal paper, cost of, 18
Comparex Information Systems, 175
comparison, between printers, difficulty of, 38-39
Compass Peripheral Systems, 175
compatibility, 47, 109, 110, 139
Compuprint, 175
Computer Aided Design (CAD), 164
Computer Aided Manufacturing (CAM), 164
computer graphics interface (CGI), 139
computer manual, 45, 56
connect, ability to, 31
consumables, 97-106
   costs of, 16, 26, 30, 104, 123, 132, 161
   use of, 25
continuous stationery, 85, 87, 88-90
contract, maintenance, 25-26, 56
copy clicks, 118
cost efficiency, 22, 24-27
cost per printed page, 33
costs, of owning printer, 10, 18, 26-27, 31, 98, 136
   high, 20, 29
   laser, 11
   low, 14, 30
Courier (typeface), 151
'cowboy' companies, 118
CPS, see characters per second
CrystalPrint, 10, 157
CrystalPrint Series II, 125-126
Current Loop standard, 48
Customer Engineers (IBM), 114
cut sheet feeder, 86, 103, 105
cut sheet work, 4, 6, 18, 84

daisywheel, impact, 7-8
daisywheel printer accessories, 105
daisywheel printers, 5, 50, 56, 130-131
data processing departments, 8, 10-11, 135
Dataproducts, 91, 103, 125, 175
   8022, 51
   band printer, 23
   inkjet, 171
   SI 480, 132, 162
Dataquest, 122, 166
Decision Data Computer (GB) Ltd, 176
default settings, 57

depreciation, 101
DeskJet, 103, 132, 152, 160
desktop publishing (DTP), 13, 24, 32, 70-72, 124, 125, 166
  software, 159
developer, 100
Diablo, 32
Diablo 630, 27, 50, 150
Diconix, 103, 131, 163, 176
Digital Equipment Co, 124, 176
Digital Research, 153
DIN (German standards body), 35, 36, 39
DIN standard letter, 33
directory tree, 52
disable switch, 48
display adaptors, interface structure for, 139
dot density, 17
  limitations, 36
dot matrix, 3-4
  impact, 3
  printers, 126-130, 136
dot size, 15
dots, pattern of, 16
dots per inch (DPI), 36, 37, 72-73
DPI, *see* dots per inch
draft printing, 4, 6, 17, 145
drivers, printer, 139
drum
  character pattern on, 20
  life of, 31
  rotating, 18
  units, 100

DTP, *see* desktop publishing
dual bin feeder, 86
dual paper hoppers, 12
duplex printer, 153
Dutch (typeface), 53
duty cycles, 22-24, 113
dye, melted from special ribbon, 16
dynamic fonts, 78

ECMA, *see* European Computer Manufacturers Association
EEC levies, 138
electrodes, number of, 17
electronic publishing, 70
electrostatic drum, 9
emulation mode, 140
emulations, 32, 49-51
endurance testing, 36
envelopes, 90, 96
Epson, 32, 57, 91, 103, 124, 125, 131, 142, 143, 176
  24-pin matrix printer, 170
  9-pin matrix printer, 170
  DFX-5000, 128, 143, 171
  FX series, 50, 143
  FX 9-pin matrix printer, 170
  FX-1000, 142
  FX-1050, 129, 143
  FX-80, 150
  FX-850, 129, 143
  GC3500, 157
  GC5000, 157
  GQ3500, 152
  GQ5000, 152

JX-80, 150
laser, 171
LQ series, 50
LQ-1050, 51, 171
LQ-1500, 148
LQ-2550, 127, 150, 171
LQ-500, 129, 146, 170
LQ-850, 128
RX-80, 142
SQ inkjet, 171
SQ-2550, 162
systems printers, 43
ergonomics, printer, 106
Erskine Printing Systems Ltd, 176
ESC/P commands, 58, 60
Europe, 37, 166
  printer market in, 30, 122
  printer revenues in, 9
European Computer Manufacturers Association (ECMA), 35, 39
European manufacturers, 39
European Printer Performance Tests (EPPTs), 34-37, 39

Facit, 34, 177
fanfold paper, 4, 29, 51, 84, 90, 135
file dumps, production of, 5
fonts, 13, 31, 52, 75-77, 79-80, 154
  dynamic, 78
  expansion, 148
  flexibility, 28, 29, 158
  mixing, 19
  options, 12
  resident, 27, 78, 150
  scalable, 125
  soft, 76
Fontware Installation Kit, 53
form printing, multi-part, 5
fourth party concept, 116-117
French, attitude to Japanese marketing practices, 35
Fujitsu, 29, 177
  24-pin matrix printers, 170, 171
  9-pin matrix printers, 170
  DL2600, 171
  DL3300, 51, 128, 147, 148
  DL3400, 128, 147, 148, 171
  DL5600, 127, 149, 150
  LED unit, 171
Futura (typeface), 76

Garamond (typeface), 76
GEM, 73
Genicom, 12, 158, 177
  6000 Series, 154
GeniScript, 154
Gestetner Data Systems Ltd, 177
Gothic (typeface), 151
graphics, 4, 12, 13, 14, 15, 16, 35, 70, 71, 73, 91, 99, 100, 130, 134, 140

flexibility, 158
high resolution, 5
high speed, 125
printer-driver standard,
  need for, 139
  test, 36-37
Graphics Printer, 50
guarantees, 25, 56, 108-110

hardware compatibility, 47
Harris Systems Ltd, 177
Helvetica (typeface), 53, 75, 76
Hermes Precisa, 34, 177
Hewlett-Packard, 10, 12, 32, 50, 91, 103, 124, 131, 156, 171, 178
  Deskjet, 152, 160-161, 170
  Laserjet, 152
  LaserJet Plus, 158
  Laserjet Series II, 153
  LaserJet Series IID, 153
  QuietJet, 170
  QuietJet+, 170
  ThinkJet, 170
Hitachi, 125, 134
Howtek, 178
  Pixelmaster, 164

IBM, 73, 124, 125, 131, 171, 178
  24-pin matrix printer, 170
  3203-5 emulation, 19
  4201 Proprinter III, 143
  4202 Proprinter III XL, 143
  4207 Proprinter X24, 148
  4208 Proprinter XL24, 148
  5204 Quickwriter, 127, 149
  Computer Users Association, 44
  connectivity to, 42-45, 157
  customer engineering role, 114-116
  Graphics, 32
  Graphics Printer, 50, 142, 148, 150
  laser and LED, 171
  laser printer for PCs, 156
  LaserPrinter E, 159
  Proprinter, 50, 142, 143, 170
  Proprinter III, 129
  Proprinter III XL, 129
  Proprinter X24, 128
  Proprinter XL, 150
  Proprinter XL24, 128, 171
  PS/2 Model 50 Z, 51
  Quickwriter, 164-165, 171
  Quietwriter III, 171
IC cards, 99
ICL, 110, 178
ICL's views, 113-114
IDC, 122, 166
IEEE-488 interface, 47, 48
impact dot matrix, 3
impact printers, market share, 122
impact technologies, 2, 3-9
industrial marking, 93
Information Technology Ltd, 178

INIT signal, 58
ink
  cartridge, 103
  magnetic, 18
  solid, 91-93
  technology, 14-16
inkjet
  non-impact, 7, 14-16, 122
  printer accessories, 102-103
  printers, 14, 56, 91, 131-132, 160-164
instruction manual, 32, 57, 89, 95
Integrex Ltd, 131, 178
interface, 31
international character set, 62
International Standards Organisation, 35, 39
ion deposition, non-impact, 20
IRMA card, 43
ISO, see International Standards Organisation

Japan, matrix printers made in, 127
Japanese companies, 138, 166
Japanese manufactur-ers, and performance testing, 37-8
Japanese manufactur-ers, marketing prac-tices of, 35
jets, clogged, 15, 131

JetScript board, 155
justification, 63-65

keyboard format, 59
keystroke combina-tions, 53
Kodak, 163
Kyocera, 78, 124, 125, 152, 158, 179
  F-1000, 156
  F-1200, 156
  F-series laser printers, 159

labelling, 6, 136
labels, 90, 96
languages, page description, 73-75
laser printers, 5, 9, 38, 39, 50, 53, 73, 79, 122, 151-160
  advantages of, 12-14
  buying a, 30-33
  compared with inkjet print-ers, 132
  consumables, 100
  and continuous station-ery, 85
  costs of running, 98
  engine, Canon, 29, 153, 155, 158
  increasing popularity of, 166
  life of, 101
  limitations of, 11-12
  low end, 151-152
  maintaining, 56-57
  non-impact, 9-14

office, 153-158
products, 124-126
sales, 124
technology, 84, 93-94
technology and markets, 123-124
what goes wrong?, 111-112
LaserJet, 10, 12, 50, 152
LaserJet Series II, 124
Laserwriter, 74
Laserwriter IINTX, 124
LCD, *see* liquid cystal display
LCS, *see* liquid crystal shutter
LED, *see* light emitting diode
letter quality, 18, 131, 141, 144, 149, 162
letters, printing, 165
light emitting diode (LED), 13-14, 29, 123, 126
lightbar select feature, 52
line matrix printing, 4-7, 134
line printers, 133-136, 166-167
  markets, 135-136
  technology, 133
liquid crystal shutter (LCS) printers, 13-14, 126
liquid crystal shutter technology, 10, 157
liquid crystal display, 123
liquid ink technologies, 14
local area network, 80, 87
logos, created in data form, 19
loopback self-test mode, 48
Lotus, 153
LQ series (Epson), 150
LQ-1050, Epson printer, 57
LQ-850, Epson printer, 57

magnetic drum, 29
magnetic imaging technology, 30
magnetic ink, 18
magnetographic, non-impact, 18-19
mainframe, printer used with, 128
Maintenance Agreement, IBM, 114
maintenance contracts, 25-26, 56, 108, 117, 118, 119, 157
maintenance, printer, 107-119
Mannesmann Tally, 125, 179
  24-pin matrix printer, 170
  340, 145
  MT290, 171
  MT86, 170
  MT91, 163
manual, computer, 45, 56
manual, instruction, 32, 57, 89, 95
market value, of band printers, 9
matrix print head, maintaining the, 55-56
matrix printers, 55

accessories, 104
technology and markets, 126-127
technology, non-impact, 17
mean time before failure (MTBF), 23
mean time between service calls (MTBSC), 23
mean time to failure (MTTF), 24
mean time to repair (MTTR), 23
measuring performance, 33-38
Memorex Telex Ltd, 179
memory expansion, 31
menus, pull down, 52
metafiles, 139
Microline 320, 142
Microline 321, 142
MicroPro International, 153
Microsoft Corporation, 153
Microsoft Windows, 73
minicomputer, printer used with, 128
MIS department, needs of, 10-11
Mita, 29, 125
Mita engines, 156
Mitsubishi Electric UK Ltd, 179
Mitsubishi G650, 102, 166
modem, 45
Motorola 68020, 158
MT 18-pin matrix printer, 171

MTBF, *see* mean time before failure
MTBSC, *see* mean time between service calls
MTTF, *see* mean time to failure
MTTR, *see* mean time to repair
multi-part forms, 5, 7, 12, 131, 144
multi-part stationery, 19
MultiMate Advantage II, 51, 52, 53
multiple bin feeders, 105
multiple bins, 142
multiple sheets, feeding in, 39

NCR Ltd, 179
near letter quality (NLQ), 4, 6, 12, 14, 17, 141, 146, 150
NEC, 127, 180
2200, 147
24-pin matrix printer, 170
Business Systems (Europe) Ltd, 180
laser and LED, 171
LED unit, 171
P2200, 129
P6 Plus, 128, 146, 147, 148
P7 Plus, 146, 147, 148, 171
Pinwriter P2200, 146, 170
networking, 80-82, 143, 166
Newbury Data Recording,

34, 180
Nixdorf, 34, 180
NLQ, *see* near letter quality
noise, printer, 4, 14, 17, 31, 146, 147, 162
non-impact laser, 123
non-impact matrix printing, 14, 17
non-impact technologies, 2, 9-20, 122
non-toxic imaging surface, 28
nozzles, 14

office lasers, 153-158
office printers, 123
Oki, 125, 151, 180
  18-pin matrix printer, 171
  9-pin matrix printer, 170
  laser, 171
  Micoline 320, 129
  Micrline 393C, 127
  Microline 292 Elite 18-pin matrix printer, 170
  Microline 320, 142, 170
  Microline 321, 142
  Microline 3891, 128
  Microline 390, 128, 148
  Microline 391, 148
  Microline 393C, 150
  models, 143
Okimate 20, 165-166
Okidata, 159
Okilaser 400, 160
Okilaser 800, 160
Olivetti, 34, 125, 148, 180
  18-pin matrix printers, 171
  24-pin matrix printer, 170
  9-pin matrix printer, 170
  daisywheel, 171
  DM 250/250L, 128, 148
  DM 250 L, 128
  PG 208 M2, 155
  TH 760S, 165, 170
Olympia, 180
on-site warranties, 108
OPC imaging surface, 29
OPC-based page printers, 28-29
operating costs, 25
operating speeds, 19
optimised logic seeking, 16
Overture 106 laser printer, 125

page description language (PDL), 73-75, 79, 158
page printers, 10
page printing, 27-30
page-oriented technology, 93
PageMaker, 70, 73
pages per hour (PPH), 35
pages per minute (PPM), 33, 34
Palatino (typeface), 76
Panasonic, 125, 130
  24-pin matrix printer, 170
  9-pin matrix printer, 170
  Industrial UK Ltd, 181
  KX-P1081, 142
  KX-P4450, 152, 156
  PageLaser 8, 157

paper, 14
  cartridges, 32
  choosing, 95-96
  feed, awkward, 146
  feed speed, 94
  hoppers, dual, 12
  jams, 51, 141
  motion, vertical, 16
  parking, 89
  perforated, 142
  quality, and print quality, 91
  requirements, 94
  special, 16
  stacking, 32
  thickness, 94
  trays, 85, 99, 105
  weight, 32, 95, 101
  width, 94
paper-handling, 144, 145
  devices, 149
  options, 15
Paper Express, 144
parallel communication, 45-46
parallel interface, built-in, 31
PCB, *see* printed circuit board
PDL Prescribe, 159
PEP, *see* Printer Enhancement Pack
perforated paper, 142
performance, measuring, 33-38, 135
performance testing, 35-38
Philips, 29, 34, 181

photocopier paper, 102
picture point size (pixel), 79
piezoelectric crystals, 15
pin feed mechanisms, 88
pin tractor feeders, 103
pixel (picture point size), 79
pixel graphics, 99
platen, split, 128
plotters, interface structure for, 139
plotting, 134
'point and shoot', 52
point size, 32
point-of-sale, 6
PostScript, 12, 32, 50-51, 73, 74, 124, 153, 160
postscript lasers, 158-159
PostScript printer, 13, 102
power stacker, 19
PPH, *see* pages per hour
PPM, *see* pages per minute
preprinted stationery, no longer necessary, 19, 27
Prescribe, 73, 74, 156
Prestige (typeface), 151
price, high, 10
prices, of printers, 170-172
pricing structures, 138
Prime Computer (UK) Ltd
print
  command, and appearance of first sheet, 34
  head, matrix, 55-56
  quality, 15
  ribbons, 101-102
  runs, high, 145

spool feature, 53
printed circuit board (PCB), 111
printer
  drivers, 51
  emulations, 32
  ergonomics, 106
  keeping a spare, 116, 117
  impact, 122
  interface structure for, 139
  life of, 31
  market, in Europe, 30
  pitfalls in comparing, 38-39
  size, 22
  technologies, impact, 2
  technologies, non-impact, 2
  vulnerability of, 113
Printer Action Table, 52
Printer Enhancement Pack (PEP), 52, 53
Printer Sharing Option, 159
printhead
  expensive, 18
  dot matrix, 4, 126
  matrix, cost of, 104
  self-adjusting, 144
printing rates, 28, 29
printing speed, 31
Printronix Ltd, 181
problems, of technology, 14, 15
programming the printer, 57-67
Proprinter, 142, 148

protocol converters, 43
publishing process, comparing DTP with conventional, 71-72
pull down menus, 52
pull feed tractors, 89
push feed tractors, 89
push/pull tractor, 89

QMS ColorScript 100, 102
QMS Europe BV, 181
QuietWriter, 101, 127
Qume, 10, 125, 181
  CrystalPrint, 51, 152, 171
  LetterPro, 170
  CrystalPrint Series II, 157

radiation emissions, 13
RAM, *see* random access memory
random access memory, 99
Rank Xerox, 182
RBS Systems Ltd, 182
reliability
  of daisywheel printers, 131
  of laser printers, 10
Remote Technical Assistance and Information Net-work (IBM), 115
resident fonts, 78
resolution, 19, 31, 72-73, 140
'Retain', *see* Remote Technical Assistance and Informa-tion Network
Retainer Service Agreement

(IBM), 114
ribbons, 101-102, 104
  colour, 105
  high cost of, 133
  quality, 17
  thermal, 17
Ricoh, 29, 125
Ricoh engine, 157
Romtec, 10, 122, 126, 131, 164
RS232/RS422 serial interface, 31
RSA, *see* Retainer Service Agreement (IBM)

sales, worldwide, of printers, 122
sans serif typefaces, 75
scanner, 70, 79
screen resolution, 28
security, 98, 105
Seikosha (UK) Ltd, 143, 182
  18-pin matrix printer, 171
  9-pin matrix printer, 170
  MP-1300AI, 129, 143
  MP-5300AI, 129
  SBP-10, 145
  SBP-10AI, 127, 145
selenium imaging surface, 28
serial communication, 45-46
serial interface, RS232/RS422, 31
serial printers, 15, 93
  market share, 122
Servicepoint (IBM), 115

servicing, 101, 107-119
Set UK Ltd, 182
Sharp, 125
Sharp engine, 156
sheet feeder, 6, 8, 18, 38, 39, 86, 142
shuttle matrix, 171
side-by-side, printing, 19
Siemens, 131, 182
soft fonts, 52, 76
software compatibility, 47, 110
software, for printers, 139
solid ink
  pellets, 132, 162
  technology, 15, 91-93
Sorbus, 116
speed, printing, 31, 133
spreadsheet, 35, 36
sprocket holes, crumbly, 51
sprocketed paper, 4
Star, 117, 125
  24-pin matrix printer, 170
  9-pin matrix printer, 170
  Laserprinter 8, 155
  LC-10 9-pin machine, 130, 142
  LC24-10, 129, 146, 170
  Micronics UK Ltd, 182
  NB-15, 171
Storage Technology, 182
Swift-64, 170
Swiss (typeface), 53
systems connection, 42-45

Tandy, 183
Taxan, 183

Techx Ltd, 183
Tektronix (UK) Ltd, 183
temperature
  rises, 36
  safe, for printers, 54
testing
  endurance, 36
  performance, 35-38
text capability, 8
text processing, 35, 36
thermal ribbon, 17
thermal transfer, 122
  accessories, 101-102
  non-impact, 16-18
  printers, 16, 56, 133, 164-166
  printers, costs of accessories, 26
  printhead, 102
  unit, 18
ThermoJet, 164
throughput (pages per month), 28, 29
  fast, 145
  measuring, 35-36
  rates, 118
Times Roman (typeface), 53, 76
toner, 9, 13, 100
toner cartridges, cost of, 136
Toshiba, 125
  24-pin matrix printer, 170
  Information Systems Ltd, 183

P351SX, 151
Toshiba Page Laser 12, 152, 156-158
Total Care programmes, 110
tractor feed mechanisms, 88
trade press, 27
twinax, 42, 43, 44
type family, 76
type sizes, 77-80
type styles, 75
typeface parameters, 32
typefaces, 32, 53
typestyles, 76-77

vector graphics, 73
Ventura Publisher, 70, 73

Wang, 124
warm-up period, 31
warranties, 108-110
Wenger Printers Ltd, 34, 183
What You See Is What You Get (WYSIWYG), 52, 70-72
WordPerfect Corporation, 153
workstations, IBM, 115
WYSIWYG, *see* What You See Is What You Get

Xerox, 29, 70
XON/XOFF protocol, 48

210 PROFITING FROM YOUR PRINTER

COMPUTER WEEKLY PUBLICATIONS

Computer Weekly is the UK's leading weekly computer newspaper which goes to over 112,000 computer professionals each week. Founded in 1967, the paper covers news, reviews and features for the computer industry. In addition, *Computer Weekly* also publishes books relevant to and of interest to its readership.

Publications to date (obtainable through your bookshop or by ringing 081-685-9435/081-661-3050) are:

The Computer Weekly Guide to Resources 1990

Our extensively indexed second Annual Guide fulfils the computer industry's need for an independent, handy, up-to-date reference review signposting and interpreting the key trends in the computer industry.

A key section this year is an in-depth independent discussion of 270 software and computer companies, invaluable for managing directors, DP managers, sales and marketing people and all executive job hunters.

Our first Annual Guide was well acclaimed: 'In spite of a plethora of guides to various aspects of the computer industry, there hasn't been one readable, comprehensive overview of the current UK scene. *Computer Weekly*'s Guide to Resources has filled the bill ... it's very good.' *The Guardian*

ISBN 1-85384-017-3   416 pages   A4 size   Price £45.00

Aliens' Guide to the Computer Industry
by John Kavanagh

In a lucid and light style, leading computer industry writer John Kavanagh discusses how the various parts of the computer industry inter-relate and what makes it tick. Complete with extensive index, the book is invaluable for all who come into contact with the computer industry.

'Business professionals who worry about their grasp of the general computing scene and do not want to be bombarded with jargon and technicalities, will get good value ... an excellent 'snapshot' of the companies, the current areas of interest and the problems' *Financial Times*

ISBN 1-85384-012-2   192 pages   A5 size   Price £9.95

COMPUTER WEEKLY PUBLICATIONS 211

Computer Jargon Explained
by Nicholas Enticknap

Following reader demand this is a totally revised, expanded and updated version of our highly successful guide to computer jargon, *Breaking the Jargon*.

This 176 page book provides the context to and discusses 68 of the most commonly used computer jargon terms. Extensively cross-indexed this book is essential reading for all computer professionals, and will be useful to many business people too.

'... a useful shield against the constant barrage of impossible language the computer business throws out' *The Independent*

'... a worthwhile investment' *Motor Transport*

ISBN 0-85384-015-7   176 pages   A5 size   Price £9.95

What To Do When a Micro Lands On Your Desk
by Glyn Moody and Manek Dubash

This book will help you get the most out of your microcomputer. It is a practical book, giving advice on how to make the transition from typewriter to micro profitably and with minimum effort.

The authors look at software - wordprocessing, databases, spreadsheets, graphics and communications - and the different types of hardware on the market. The book contains valuable information on training, health and security, and legal matters including the Data Protection Act, operating systems, the history of the computer, the current micro scene and the future.

ISBN 1-85384-011-4   296 pages   A5 size   Price £14.95

Considering Computer Contracting? by Michael Powell

This is a completely revised and updated edition of the highly successful book which has helped many computer professionals break loose from being employees to working freelance, in some cases doubling their salaries.

There is information on: who uses computer contractors and why; what it takes to become a contract worker; how to find your first contract; how to keep your skills updated; forming your own company and handling finances; contract agencies.

ISBN 1-85384-022-X   176 pages   A5 size   Price £12.95

212 PROFITING FROM YOUR PRINTER

Hitchhikers' Guide to Electronics in the '90s by David Manners

Developments in electronics underpin not only the computer industry but also the whole of modern society. This book is essential if DP and IT professionals are to identify trends that will affect all our jobs in the 1990s.

David Manners, an awarding winning senior editor on *Electronics Weekly* newspaper, lucidly explains the electronics industry and its key products and discusses its central role and implications to industry in the 1990s.

Essential reading for IT staff, marketing and sales directors, strategic planners and all interested in the future of the IT industry.

ISBN 1-85384-020-3   224 pages   A5 size   Price £12.95

A Simple Introduction to Data and Activity Analysis
by Rosemary Rock-Evans

Successful analysis of business operations is a prerequisite to building any computer system within a company. Whereas many existing books approach this topic from an academic point of view, this one is the fruit of years of practical analysis in blue chip companies.

Rosemary Rock-Evans is a leading consultant. Her first book on this topic for *Computer Weekly*, published in 1981, is now out of print. However, the considerable demand within the industry for this book has resulted in this totally revised and updated version.

This book is essential reading for all analysts in the computer industry, and is also recommended for students to give them a taste of the real world of analysis.

ISBN 1-85384-001-7   272 pages   A4 size   Price £24.95

Open Systems: The Basic Guide to OSI and its Implementation
by Peter Judge

We recognise the need for a concise, clear guide to the complex area of computer standards, untrammelled by jargon and with appropriate and comprehensible analogies to simplify this difficult topic. This book, a unique collaboration between *Computer Weekly* and the magazine *Systems International*, steers an independent and neutral path through this contentious area and is essential for users and suppliers and is required reading for all who come into contact with the computer industry.

ISBN 1-85384-009-2   192 pages   A5 size   Price £12.95

COMPUTER WEEKLY PUBLICATIONS 213

IT Perspectives Conference: The Future of the IT Industry

Many nuggets of strategic thought are contained in this carefully edited transcript of the actual words spoken by leading IT industry decision makers at *Computer Weekly*'s landmark conference held late in 1987. The conference was dedicated to discussing current and future directions the industry is taking from four perspectives: supplier perspectives; communications perspectives; user perspectives and future perspectives.

'... makes compelling reading for those involved in the business computer industry' *The Guardian*

'... thought-provoking points and some nice questions put to speakers at the end' *Daily Telegraph*

ISBN 1-85384-008-4   224 pages   A4 size   Price £45.00

Computer Weekly Book of Puzzlers
Compiled by Jim Howson

Test your powers of lateral thinking with this compendium of 187 of the best puzzles published over the years in *Computer Weekly*. The detailed explanations of how solutions are reached make this a useful guide to recreational mathematics. No computer is needed to solve these fascinating puzzles.

'... a pleasant collection of puzzles exercises for computer freaks. Actually probably fewer than half the puzzles here need a computer solution ...' *Laboratory Equipment Digest*

ISBN 1-85384-002-5   160 pages   A5 size   Price £6.95

Women in Computing by Judith Morris

Written by a respected former editor of several computer magazines, this book reflects the upsurge in awareness of the important role women can play in helping to stem the critical skills shortage within the computer industry.

The book addresses women's issues in a practical and sensible way and is aimed at all business women both in the computer industry or who work with computers. Contains much practical advice, including the names and addresses of useful organisations, and a valuable further reading list.

ISBN 1-85384-004-1   128 pages   A5 size   Price £9.95

214 PROFITING FROM YOUR PRINTER

How to Get Jobs in Microcomputing
by John F Charles

As micros proliferate throughout organisations, opportunities for getting jobs in the micro area are expanding rapidly. The author, who has worked with micros in major organisations, discusses how to get started in microcomputing, describes the different types of job available, and offers tips and hints based on practical experience. Ideal for recent graduates, and those already working with minicomputers or mainframes, who are looking towards a career in micros.

ISBN 1-85384-010-6   160 pages   A5 size   Price £6.95

Low Cost PC Networking
by Mike James

The whole area of PC networking is taking off rapidly now. Can you afford to be left behind?

Mike James' Low Cost PC Networking shows how networking revolutionises the way we use PCs and the tasks that they perform. It also explains how networking goes further than simply linking PCs, and how it enables you to integrate your operations to transform your business.

Chapters cover every aspect of networking, from planning your network and selecting the hardware and software to applications, technicalities and contacts.

ISBN 0-434-90897-5   256 pages   246 x 188 mm   Price £16.95

Selling Information Technology: A Practical Career Guide
by Eric Johnson

Selling in IT requires more skill and creativity than selling in any other profession. This essential handbook for IT sales people explains why and provides practical down-to-earth advice on achieving the necessary extra skills.

A collaboration between *Computer Weekly* and the *National Computing Centre*, this book discusses practical career issues, general IT sales issues, and key IT industry developments.

ISBN 0-85012-684-3   244 pages   144 x 207 mm   Price £12.50